4399

J915
K
c.1

Koenig, Marion.
The travels of Marco Polo. Illustrated by Mario Logli and Gabriele Santini. New York, Golden Press [1966] c1964.

77 p. col. illus., fold. col. map. 29 cm.

1. Polo, Marco, 1254-1323?—Juvenile literature. I. Title.

G370.P9K57 j 915 66-5512

Library of Congress [2]

RBP

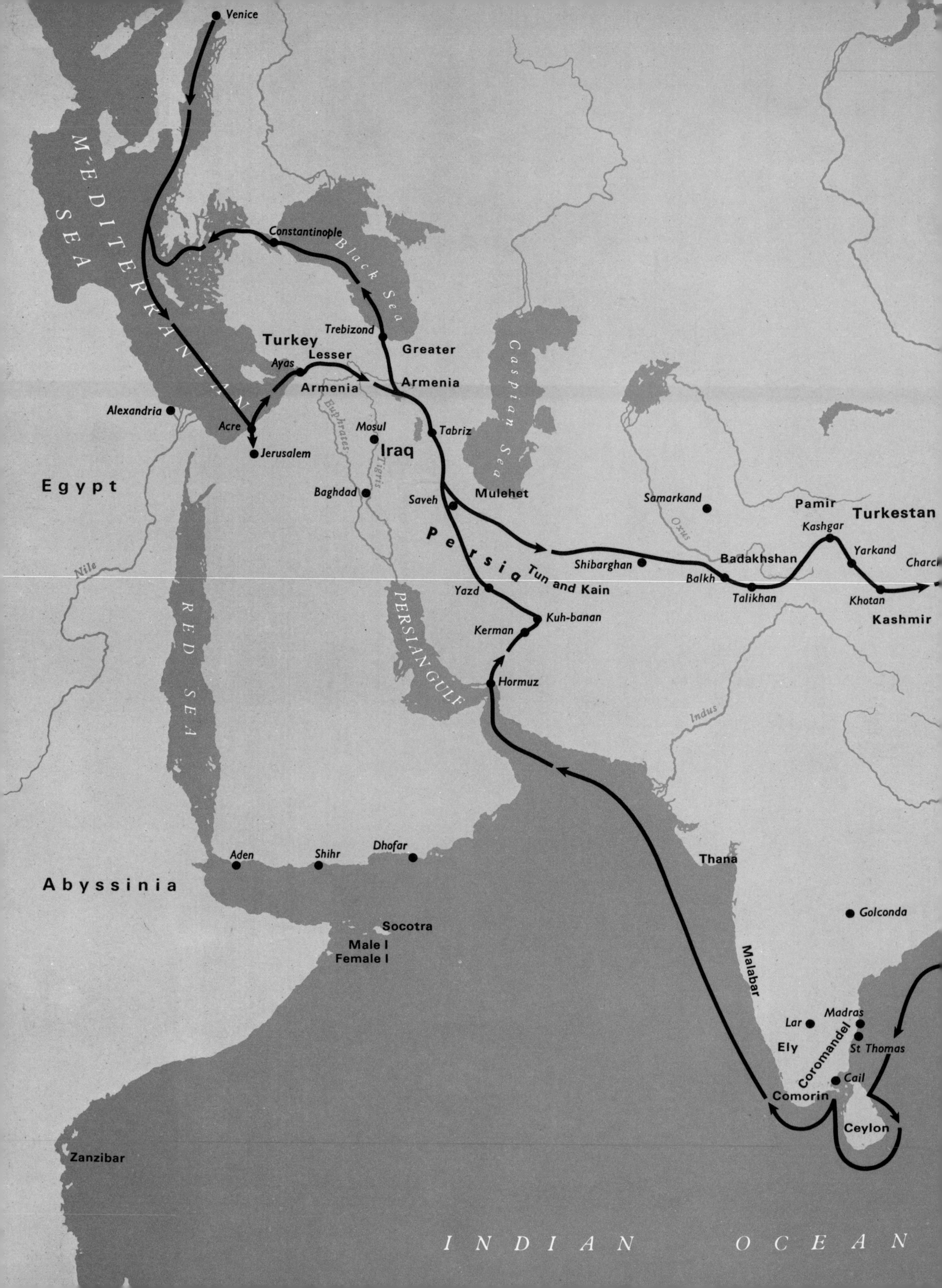
Venice
MEDITERRANEAN SEA
Constantinople
Black Sea
Trebizond
Turkey
Greater
Armenia
Lesser
Armenia
Ayas
Alexandria
Acre
Jerusalem
Mosul
Iraq
Euphrates
Tigris
Baghdad
Tabriz
Caspian Sea
Egypt
Saveh
Mulehet
Persia
Samarkand
Oxus
Pamir
Turkestan
Kashgar
Yarkand
Badakhshan
Shibarghan
Balkh
Talikhan
Khotan
Kashmir
Tun and Kain
Yazd
Kuh-banan
Kerman
Nile
RED SEA
PERSIAN GULF
Hormuz
Indus
Aden
Shihr
Dhofar
Thana
Abyssinia
Socotra
Male I
Female I
Golconda
Malabar
Lar
Madras
Ely
Coromandel
St Thomas
Cail
Comorin
Ceylon
Zanzibar
INDIAN OCEAN

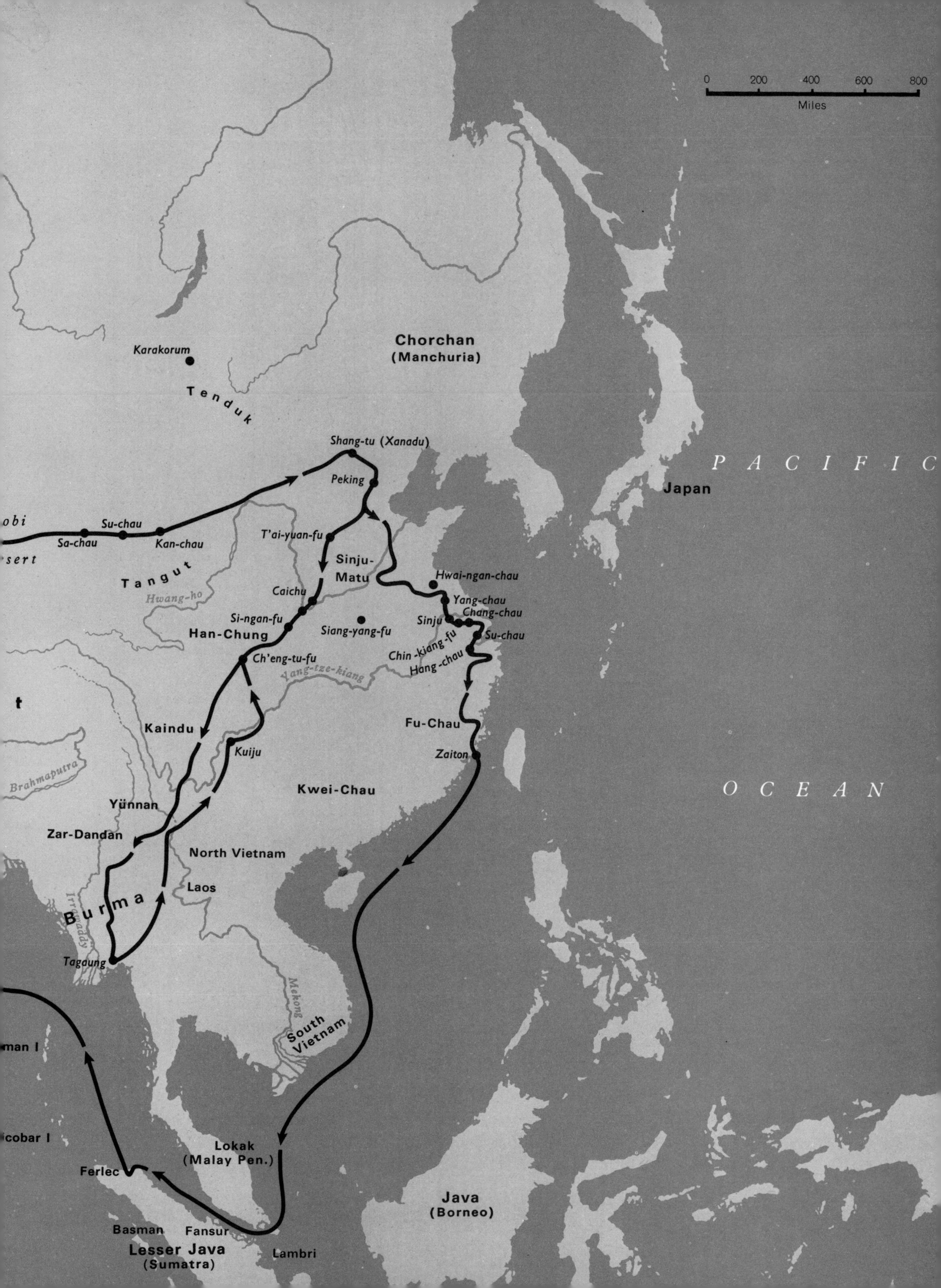

0
200
400
600
800
Miles
Chorchan
(Manchuria)
Karakorum
Tenduk
Shang-tu (Xanadu)
Peking
PACIFIC
Japan
obi
sert
Su-chau
Sa-chau
Kan-chau
T'ai-yuan-fu
Sinju-
Matu
Tangut
Hwang-ho
Hwai-ngan-chau
Caichu
Yang-chau
Si-ngan-fu
Sinju
Chang-chau
Han-Chung
Siang-yang-fu
Su-chau
Ch'eng-tu-fu
Chin-kiang-fu
Hang-chau
Yang-tze-kiang
t
Kaindu
Fu-Chau
Kuiju
Zaiton
Brahmaputra
Kwei-Chau
OCEAN
Yünnan
Zar-Dandan
North Vietnam
Laos
Burma
Irrawaddy
Tagaung
Mekong
South
Vietnam
man I
cobar I
Lokak
(Malay Pen.)
Ferlec
Java
(Borneo)
Basman
Fansur
Lesser Java
(Sumatra)
Lambri

BY MARION KOENIG
ILLUSTRATED BY MARIO LOGLI AND GABRIELE SANTINI

THE TRAVELS

Printed in the U.S.A. by Western Printing and Lithographing Company
Published by Golden Press, Inc., New York

OF MARCO POLO

GOLDEN PRESS NEW YORK

INTRODUCTION

This is the story of a remarkable series of overland voyages which took place over five hundred years ago.

Three merchants, Niccolo, Maffeo and Marco Polo, traveled through deserts and over mountains, facing terrible dangers, until they reached China—the first Europeans ever to do so. Once they got there they made friends with one of the most powerful rulers of that time, the great Mongol emperor, Khubilai Khan. He gave them interesting jobs to do which made them very rich and helped them to go on traveling all over China and other parts of the Far East which nobody in Europe knew existed.

The Great Khan grew so fond of them that they stayed with him for twenty years. In fact they found it very hard to get permission to leave him. In the end they became quite desperate because, for one thing, they badly wanted to see their families again and, for another, they knew that the Great Khan was an old man of seventy-one and could not go on living for much longer. And they knew that once he was dead all the people who had been jealous of the favors which he had shown the Polo family would at once try to get their own back on Niccolo, Maffeo and Marco.

Just when they had given up all hope some nobles arrived at the Great Khan's court from Persia. They had been sent by their king, Arghun Khan, who was not only a vassal of the Great Khan but one of his close relatives as well. Arghun Khan's wife had died and now he wanted to marry another Mongol princess. Of course the Great Khan was only too happy to send one of his princesses to Persia. The question was how to get her there. At that time it was much too uncomfortable and dangerous for a young princess to travel to Persia by the overland routes. Marco Polo saw his chance. He told Khubilai Khan that he and Niccolo and Maffeo knew the way to Persia by sea, and he begged the Great Khan to let them take the princess there. The Great Khan was not very happy about this arrangement but in the end he agreed that it would be the best way out of the difficulty. So he gave them all the ships and food they needed and then they set off.

After a very trying journey—of the six hundred people who set out (not counting the sailors) only 18 reached Persia—they were able to give the princess not to Arghun Khan, who had meanwhile died, but to his son. Then, traveling via Trebizond and Constantinople, the Polo family at last reached Venice, after being away for twenty-four years.

As was only to be expected, nobody recognized them at first, and it was only when they slit open the linings of their strange Mongol clothes and showed everybody the costly jewels which poured out, that people began to listen to their story.

Soon everything returned to normal. Maffeo, Niccolo and Marco went back to live in their old home, and it was not long before they were carrying on their old trade as merchants in precious stones. But just when the first excitement over their return was beginning to die down, Marco Polo got involved in another adventure.

He was making a business trip to Layas in a Venetian merchant ship, which was one of twenty-five ships sailing in convoy, when fifteen Genoese merchantmen hove into sight and attacked the Venetian fleet. Rivalry for sea power was keen between the different Mediterranean seafaring states in those days and none was so fierce as the rivalry between Venice and Genoa. On this occasion the Genoese, though greatly outnumbered by the Venetians, carried the day and took prisoner all the Venetian crews, Marco Polo among them.

So, a year after his return from China, Marco was languishing in a Genoese prison, and there he stayed for three years.

Now it so happened that among his fellow prisoners was a man called Rustichello. He was a writer of popular romances. Rustichello and Marco soon struck up a friendship and Marco suggested that they should pass the long, boring hours in prison by writing a full account of his travels. Rustichello was only too pleased to fall in with this suggestion and the two set to work. That was how the famous book came to be written, the book which everyone now knows as THE TRAVELS OF MARCO POLO, but which was then called *Liber Milionis* (the book of a thousand things).

When Marco was released he took the book back with him to Venice, where it

The Great Khan gave them all the ships and food they would need for their journey to Persia with the princess

was read by everybody who could get hold of it. Soon it was the talk of the town and it was being copied out and sent all over Europe (there was no printing in those days). But people read it purely because it was an exciting story. Nobody believed Marco Polo could possibly have seen the things he said he had. It was a long time before anybody took the book seriously. When they did, other explorers, like Columbus, started trying to find the seaway to the Far East where there was so much wealth just waiting to be brought back to Europe. And these explorers, though they did not find the sea route to China right away, did find all sorts of other new lands instead. So Marco Polo's book had an enormous effect on the course of history and is one of the landmarks of our Western civilization.

Now that you know something about Marco Polo, and how his book came to be written, here is the story of his travels.

Hulagu Khan ordered the caliph and his treasure to be walled up together in a high tower

THE JOURNEY TO XANADU

Over five hundred years ago three men set sail from Acre, in Palestine, for Ayas in an eastern corner of the Mediterranean. They were the Venetian merchants, Niccolo and Maffeo Polo, and Niccolo's seventeen-year-old son Marco. This was the first stage of a journey which was to take them more than three years. They were traveling to the court of the Great Khan of all the Mongols at Xanadu in distant China.

In those days it was not possible to buy a ticket and leave all the arrangements to a travel agency. Travelers had to find their own way stage by stage. They had to take food with them and be able to defend themselves against any bandits or wild animals who might attack them.

Another difficulty was that Niccolo, Maffeo and Marco Polo did not know the country through which they would be traveling. But they had with them the Great Khan's safe conduct, a golden tablet, ordering every person throughout his lands to see that they came to no harm and help them on their way.

After they had landed in Ayas, the Polo family bought horses and enough food to last them for many days. Then they set off on the long journey across Asia.

It was a particularly dangerous journey to make at that time. The Mongols who ruled over Iraq were at war with the Egyptians and there was a good chance that the Polos would get mixed up in the fighting. But Niccolo and Maffeo decided to take the risk and go on.

Look at the map in the front of the book to see which way they went. To reach the main road from the Black Sea to the Persian Gulf they had to go to Armenia and then travel south to Tabriz. From Tabriz the road led to Kerman, where it divided—one way leading to Hormuz on the Persian Gulf, the other leading northwards again.

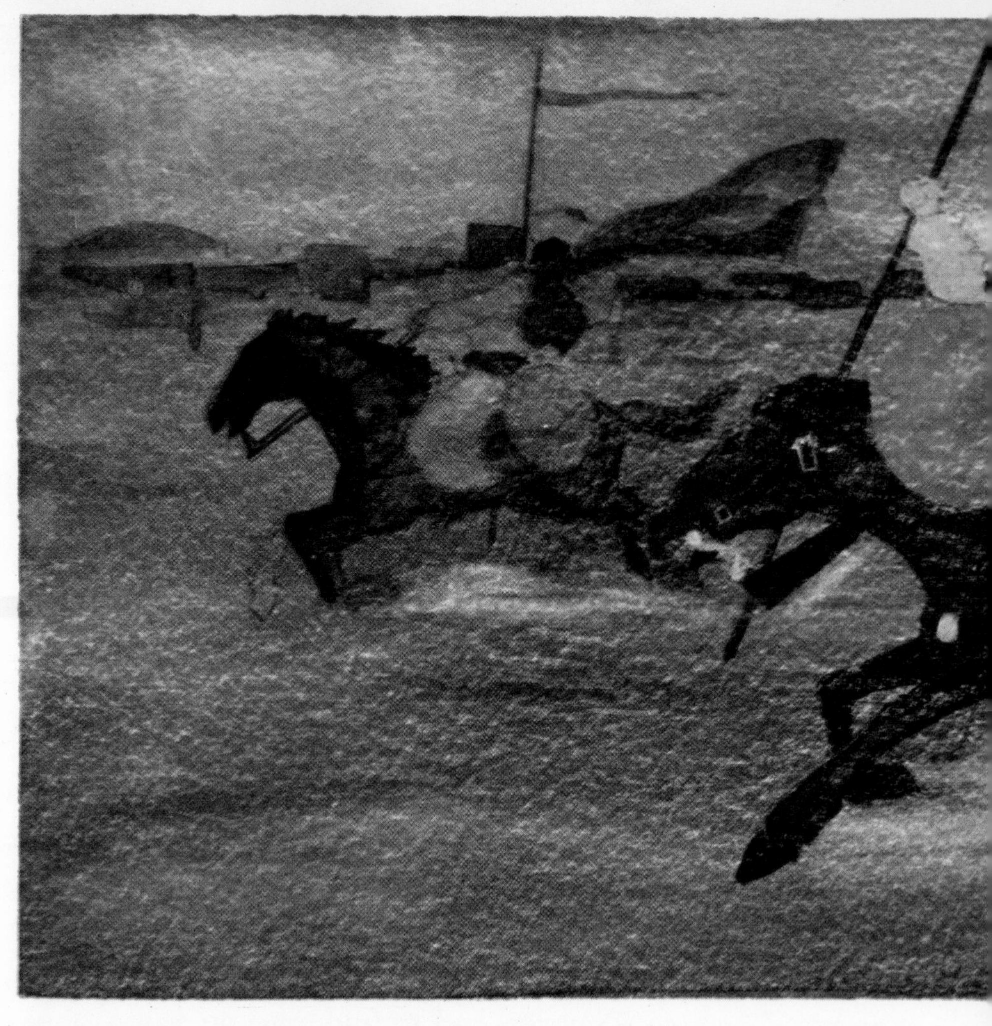

The storm was at its height when they heard the attacking cries of the fierce Karaunas

Everything that Marco Polo saw seemed so exciting and strange that he never forgot what he had seen and later wrote an account of his journeying.

South to Hormuz

The travelers passed Ararat, the high mountain on which, it was said, Noah's ark had come to rest after the Great Flood.

They saw oil gushing out of the ground and Marco found out that it could not be used for cooking, though it was very good as fuel and some people thought it could be used for curing skin diseases too.

In Armenia they visited the monastery of St. Leonard. It stood on the shores of a miraculous lake. All the year round there was not a fish to be seen until the first day of Lent, when the lake was suddenly full of them. Then, on Easter Day, all the fish disappeared again.

They rode past the lands of the Arabs, a people who followed the Muslim faith

and were hostile to Christians. They were known in Europe as the Saracens. The Polo family passed Baghdad in the distance but did not go near the town.

Marco remembered and wrote down two stories he had been told about the great city of Baghdad.

Baghdad

Years ago the Caliph of Baghdad had decided to get rid of the Christians. So he called all of them into his presence.

"It is written in your Gospel that if there is one Christian with faith as large as a grain of mustard seed, he can move a mountain," said the cunning caliph. "I am sure there must be that much faith among so many of you. I give you ten days to move that mountain. If you can't do it, I shall have you all killed."

The Christians were very frightened indeed. They gathered around their archbishop and prayed for eight days and eight nights. Suddenly an angel appeared to one of the bishops in a vision.

The shoemaker knelt down to pray

"Go to the shoemaker," the angel said. "He will save you all."

The bishop knew at once whom he meant. There was a shoemaker living in Baghdad who led a very holy life. He was loved by everybody. The bishop hurried off to see him. But the shoemaker did not think he was at all good enough to take part in a miracle. The bishop had to talk to him for a long time before he would consent to try.

On the tenth day all the Christians went out in procession onto the plain opposite the mountain. When they were all there, the shoemaker knelt down to pray.

The caliph stood near by with his armed men, ready to kill the Christians, when suddenly the mountain began to crumble and move. The caliph and his men were so terrified that many of them became Christians at once.

The other story Marco Polo wrote down described the Mongols' conquest of Baghdad, sixteen years before.

At that time, Baghdad had been ruled by a caliph who was as mean as he was wealthy. When he heard that the Mongol horsemen, under Hulagu Khan, were riding towards Baghdad and would soon attack the town, he called on his hundred thousand soldiers to defend it. But the Mongols fought so fiercely that they had soon taken the town by storm.

The Mongols were more interested in fighting and horses than they were in hoarding up treasure.

"Why did you pile up all this wealth?" Hulagu Khan asked the caliph. "What did you mean to do with it all?"

The miserly caliph did not know what to say in reply. Hulagu thought the idea of piling up treasure was so stupid that he had the caliph and his treasure walled up together in a high tower. He told him to eat the treasure if he felt hungry.

From that time on, Baghdad had been ruled by the Mongols.

Marco was delighted with this story. The caliphs of Baghdad had been Saracens and the Saracens had been the enemies of the Christian crusaders for centuries. The Muslim Saracens looked on all non-Muslims with contempt—they called them infidels—and were particularly hostile towards the Christians, who kept on trying to recapture the Holy Places from them. This story made him even more interested in the Mongols, who were later to become such good friends of his.

The Fire Worshipers of Saveh

Inside the casket the Magi found a stone

The travelers rode south down the road to Saveh. Here Marco was taken to see the tombs of the three wise men, Caspar, Melchior and Balthazar, who had so many hundreds of years earlier gone to Bethlehem to offer their gifts of gold, frankincense and myrrh to the baby Christ.

There was a legend in those parts that the baby Christ accepted all their gifts and in return gave the three wise men, or Magi, a locked casket.

On their way home the Magi opened the casket. Inside they found a stone which Christ had given them to remind them to rest firm in their faith. But they didn't understand and in their disappointment threw the stone into a nearby well. At once a great flame came down from the sky, entered the well and continued to burn there.

Then the Magi were sorry. They took some of the fire and carried it to one of their temples, where it was worshiped as a sacred fire.

From Saveh to Hormuz

From Saveh the road led onto Kerman across a fertile plain where there was good hunting, for the woods were filled with partridges and quails.

When they had passed Kerman, however, they joined a large caravan of merchants so that they would feel safer crossing the hot desert which lay before them. And here the Polo family had a frightening adventure.

The sky darkened and an eerie silence fell over the land. Then, all of a sudden, a blinding sandstorm swept over them. They could hardly breathe and were completely at the mercy of the powerful wind.

In that suffocating darkness they lost sight of the other travelers and cowered against their beasts, waiting for the storm to pass.

The storm was at its height when they heard the attacking cries of a fierce band of robbers, who were known as the Karaunas. These robbers carried off or killed many of the people with whom the Polo family were traveling and Marco Polo only just managed to escape being captured himself.

Marco believed that the Karaunas could call up a sandstorm by magic and that they always attacked in this way.

When the Polos reached Hormuz they tried to find a ship which would take them to China by sea. But they saw that all the ships were too small, so they decided to go back to Kerman and take the northern road which led through the land of Persia.

From Hormuz to Talikhan

The northern road ran across a vast desert in which there was no fresh water for a hundred miles. They had to carry all the water and food they would need with them. It took them seven days to cross this bleak country to the next town. Then they had to ride for another eight days until they came to a cooler and more fertile region. While they were resting here after their exhausting journey, the inhabitants told Marco Polo about the Old Man of the Mountain, who had once lived in a country near by called Mulehet.

This extraordinary person laid out a beautiful garden in a valley between two mountains. He planted fruit trees and stocked the grounds with many different kinds of animals and birds. A pavilion, decorated with gold, was set up near three rivers, one filled with milk, the second with honey and the third with wine. The Old Man's idea was to make the garden as nearly like his idea of paradise as he could.

He did so for a curious reason. He ruled his people by fear. If anybody refused to obey his commands or plotted against him, the Old Man would send a young soldier to murder him. These young men were so reckless that they would dare any odds to carry out their task. This is how the Old Man worked on them to make them kill without fear.

Every now and then he would give one of his young soldiers a draught of a drug called hashish. Then, while the young man was asleep, he would be carried into the Old Man's garden. When he awoke and saw all the beautiful things around him, he would believe he was in paradise.

After he had spent some time here in perfect happiness he would again be given a draught of hashish and carried back to the Old Man's court.

The young soldier was so unhappy to have lost the joys of paradise that he would eagerly carry out any murder the Old Man ordered him to commit, for the Old Man always promised that if he died he would go straight back to paradise, and if he lived he would see that his angels carried him there just the same.

Because of the hashish which they drank these young men were called assassins, a word which comes from the Arabic *hashshashin* or hashish-eater.

After resting near this place, the Polo family traveled via Shibarghan to the city of Balkh, which marked the eastern limit of the kingdom of the Persian Mongols.

From here they had to ride across a vast stretch of open country which was completely deserted.

They did not meet a single person during the twelve days they spent riding across it.

Later, when they at last reached a village again, they discovered the reason why nobody lived in that empty land. The people had all fled into the mountains to escape from the bandits and invaders who used to attack them.

The Old Man of the Mountain had laid out a beautiful garden

Across the Roof of the World

The next town they stopped at was called Talikhan. Beyond Talikhan the mountains which the Mongols called the Roof of the World rose steeply in their path. They had a great struggle to get up them.

In the midst of the mountains, on a grassy plain, lay a country called Badakhshan, ruled by a king who Marco believed was descended from Alexander the Great. They rested in this peaceful place for some time.

Marco noticed that the men dressed in animal skins, but the women wore wide trousers, made out of the finest linen, in order to look fatter—for a plump woman was thought beautiful in those parts.

The worst struggle was yet to come. Beyond Badakhshan the mountains rose ever more steeply. With great difficulty the Polos followed the course of the River Oxus until they reached a vast tableland. Here, said Marco enthusiastically, were the best pasturelands in the world. Wild sheep, with long curved horns, grazed all over the plain in large numbers, and he was interested to see that the shepherds ate their food out of bowls which they had carved from the horns of these sheep. But the cold was intense and there were no villages where they could find shelter. They were very glad to reach Kashgar, a town east of Samarkand.

In Kashgar the townsmen were still talking of a great miracle which had taken place not many years before.

When Chagatai, the brother of the great Genghis Khan, became a Christian, he built a church to St. John the Baptist there. In the center of the church, under a column supporting the whole roof, the Christians laid a beautiful stone which they had taken from the Saracens.

Then Chagatai died, and his son, who was not a Christian, succeeded him. At once the Saracens demanded the return of their stone and the new ruler ordered the Christians to return it within two days or it would be the worse for them.

The Christians did not know what to do. If the stone were to be removed the column would have to be lifted and this would make the church fall into ruins. But when the morning came on which the stone had to be given back, the column moved by itself and the stone lay free.

The women wore wide trousers

Chagatai's son was so impressed by this miracle, which he regarded as an omen, that the stone was not removed.

To Kashmir and on to the Gobi Desert

The shepherds ate their food out of bowls carved from the horns of their sheep

From Kashgar the travelers rode south past Yarkand, and after seven days reached the borders of Kashmir.

Although he does not say so in his book, Marco Polo must have visited Kashmir, for he describes the people and their way of life in interesting detail.

"The people who live here are thin and have brown skins," he wrote. "Their women are very beautiful."

He mentioned that they were not the vassals of some great emperor but an independent people ruled by their own king. This should have meant that they were a nation of powerful warriors who could frighten away any invaders who wished to attack them. Yet Marco Polo found that they were a gentle people who thought it a sin to kill animals or shed blood.

Marco Polo was amazed to see that the inhabitants of Kashmir worshiped idols. In fact they were Buddhists, but it seemed a very strange religion to him.

He was amazed when he saw them do things which seemed to him impossible, and wrote in his book that they practiced magic and were so good at it that they could make their idols speak, change the weather and do all sorts of other remarkable things.

Everywhere he went, he was impressed when he saw the enormous monasteries which had been built by the devoted followers of this religion. He was surprised to see that the monks who lived in them wore tonsures just like the Dominican and Franciscan friars he had known in Europe, and he met many people in the world outside the monasteries who had given up all their possessions to worship the Lord Buddha in poverty and prayer.

Then the Polo family traveled a thousand miles from one oasis to the next, from Khotan to Pem, from Pem to Charchan and from Charchan at last to Lop, the oasis which lay at the entrance to the great desert of Lop, which is also known as the Gobi Desert.

From Lop to Xanadu

Here they stayed for some time, resting and getting up their strength for the next part of their journey. They would have to travel for one month across a sandy waste in which there was no game to be hunted for food and only a small well at the end of each day's journey to supply them with water.

While they were crossing the desert, Marco Polo noticed a very strange thing. He said they could hear spirit voices calling them, and sometimes the sound of musical instruments, particularly the beating of drums.

He found out that many travelers had been lost because they had followed the sound of the voices. Lured further and further away from the main party, they were left wandering miles from the known roads through the desert until they died of exhaustion and thirst.

However, Marco Polo and his party were not led astray by the spirit voices. A month after they had set out across the desert they reached the town of Sa-chau on the other side. The people here were also Buddhists, and Marco described how figures of horses, rams, camels and money were cut out of paper and burned with the body of a dead man, so that they would be of use to him in the next world.

From Sa-chau they traveled east through the mountainous country of Tangut to Su-chau. The chief export of this region appeared to be rhubarb. It grew plentifully there.

Marco Polo was told that it was dangerous to travel too far into the mountains because of a herb which, if eaten by cattle, deer or horses, was said to make them lose their hooves. Musk deer roamed wild through the countryside but they were able to recognize the herb and avoid eating it. The musk deer is a graceful animal rather like a gazelle and it was one of the Mongols' favorite animals.

From Su-chau the travelers rode to Kan-chau, the splendid capital city of Tangut, which lay by the Great Wall. There were many beautiful Buddhist temples, as well as three Christian churches and a few Saracen mosques, in this old Chinese city.

The Polo family stayed in Kan-chau for some time waiting for word from the Great Khan. Then, one day, orders came for them to go on, so off they set again and, after traveling north for sixty days, they were met by the Great Khan's messengers and brought to Khubilai Khan at his favorite summer residence in Shang-tu or Xanadu. Their long, hard journey was over at last.

THE MONGOLS

Khubilai Khan was fifty-one years old when Marco Polo and his family arrived in Xanadu. When they were taken into his presence Marco was at once struck by the splendor of the Great Khan's surroundings and the gentle courtesy of his manner.

The people in Europe had long feared the savage Mongol horsemen who left death and destruction behind them wherever they went. On his way to Xanadu Marco had seen for himself the heaps of scorched rubble which were all the Mongols had left of the towns they had conquered. Although his father and uncle had told him of the marvels he would see at the court of Khubilai Khan, it must have come as a surprise to find that the warrior king of a barbarous people was, in fact, a man of such noble bearing, surrounded by every luxury.

The Herdsmen of the Steppes

Only seventy or eighty years ago the Mongols had lived in scattered tribes which roamed the steppes or grasslands of Manchuria in northern China. They did not build houses or till the land. They were herdsmen, living near their animals in tents which could easily be set up or taken down as their horses and sheep moved on to fresh pastures.

They did not have a lord of their own. They paid tribute to a man whom Marco Polo calls Prester John, but who was probably Togrul, the ruler of the powerful Kerait tribe.

The Mongols were expert horsemen

Then gradually the numbers of the wandering herdsmen began to increase. Soon there were so many of them that Prester John became afraid. He ordered them to leave the Manchurian grasslands. Since they were split up into tribes and had no leader they were forced to submit.

They moved away into the northern desertlands where they had a very hard time trying to find food for themselves and their animals. They would all have starved to death if it had not been for one man, who went from tribe to tribe encouraging the people. He inspired the men to join him and trained them until he had made them into the best fighting force that had ever been known. The name of this man was Genghis Khan.

Under Genghis Khan the Mongols were united for the first time. Now they felt strong enough to get better pastures for themselves. Their first move was against Prester John.

The battle between Genghis Khan and Prester John

Genghis Khan started off peaceably enough. He sent messengers to Prester John asking for his daughter's hand in marriage. But when he heard what the messengers had to say Prester John was angry.

"Has Genghis Khan no shame?" he exclaimed disdainfully. "How can he think that I would give my daughter to a common Mongol? Tell him that I would rather burn my daughter at the stake than give her to him."

The messengers rode back to Genghis Khan and reported what had happened. Then Genghis Khan flew into a great passion, for he was a proud man.

"Prester John shall pay dearly for this insult," he cried. "He shall soon learn what a common Mongol can do."

At once he called together his great army and at their head rode to the plain of Tenduk, in Mongolia. From Tenduk he sent word to Prester John that he was waiting to do battle with him there.

Prester John came swiftly to the plain with his fighting men, and both armies lay in camp facing each other. Then they rested so that they would be ready to fight.

That night Genghis Khan called his astrologers and asked them to tell him who would win the battle. The astrologers took a cane, split it halfway down the center and bent one half in the direction of Genghis Khan and the other in the direction of Prester John.

"He shall win whose cane springs back on top of the other," they declared. Then they stood back, and everybody saw the cane of Genghis Khan spring back onto that of Prester John. And Genghis Khan was filled with joy.

One of the animals which the Mongols valued was the musk deer

The next day the battle took place. There was fierce fighting on both sides and many men were killed. But late that afternoon Prester John was slain and his army routed. The Mongols had won.

When the Mongols found that nobody could stand against them they began to like fighting for its own sake. In twelve years they had conquered the whole of Cathay in northern China. Then they determined to conquer the whole world.

Genghis Khan died in battle in 1227. He was succeeded by five Khans, the last of them, Khubilai, being called the Great Khan because he was the most mighty. But long before Khubilai Khan became the overlord of the Mongols, the armies of Genghis Khan had conquered nearly the whole of Eurasia.

The Mongol life

In spite of their conquests, the Mongols never gave up their simple way of life.

They grazed their flocks in the valleys during winter and on the high mountains in summer.

They hunted the many different kinds of game. One of the animals which the Mongols valued greatly was the musk deer.

They built tents out of wood covered with felt which could be taken down and

The Great Khan used to take a leopard on the crupper of his horse when he went hunting

set up wherever they went. Their wagons, too, were covered with felt to keep out the rain.

The men's work was hunting and fighting. The women did all the other work.

The god they worshiped was called Natigai. Felt images of Natigai and his wife and children stood in all their tents and were given offerings of food before every meal.

They relied entirely on their herds for all that they needed in the way of food and clothing, although after a battle they would seize the rich furs and silks of the enemy, for they loved finery.

Like gypsies, they had a contempt for people who lived in houses and tilled the land. They didn't understand them at all. That is why they destroyed the towns whenever they could.

Marco Polo described them as being very brave and highly disciplined in battle. He said that one of their favorite ways of fighting was to pretend to run away. Then, while they were riding off at top speed, they would turn round in their saddles and shoot down all the horses of their pursuers. When their enemies were on foot they would turn and slaughter them too.

In order to be able to do this they had to be skillful archers, for it is not easy to shoot accurately from a galloping horse. They also had to be expert horsemen. The Mongol was almost tireless too. He could ride for ten days without eating or resting. When he became faint for lack of food he would cut a vein in his horse's neck and drink the blood which spurted out.

With such soldiers it was quite possible to conquer the world.

But Khubilai Khan had left this life behind him. The Chinese had shown him another kind of life. Because of the Chinese he had learned to appreciate beautiful things and to be interested in new ideas.

The palaces of Khubilai Khan

Khubilai Khan built a palace in Peking and so gave up the wandering life of his ancestors. However, he had not become quite Chinese. In the courtyard of this palace he sowed prairie grass to remind him of the life from which he had come, and whenever he had a chance he went away from cities to hunt. That is why he was so fond of his summer palace in Xanadu. It lay far to the north on the borders of the land from which the Mongols had originally come. It reminded him of his old free life.

The palace at Xanadu was built by Chinese architects. It was made of marble and carved with statues of animals and flowers. Inside, the rooms were gilded, and sparkled with precious stones.

The palace was surrounded by a high wall. Outside this wall lay sixteen miles of parkland which was partly laid out in gardens, with lawns watered by fountains and streams, and partly as a deer park for the Khan's private hunting parties. The Khan used to hunt the smaller deer with his falcons. He would pursue the larger animals with a leopard, which he would take with him on the crupper of his horse.

In the middle of the park stood a pavilion made entirely of bamboos. The strips of bamboo on the roof were laid like tiles and lacquered so that the rain could not get through. Inside, the bamboo was gilded and decorated with beautiful designs of birds and other animals. The pavilion was held up by two hundred silken cords so that it could be taken down and set up wherever the Khan wished.

As he got to know him better, Marco Polo began to admire Khubilai Khan more than anybody else in the world. He learned that Khubilai had not been able to stay Great Khan without fighting the people who envied him his position. In addition to being a most cultivated prince, Khubilai Khan was also a strong and warlike commander.

First he had to fight his own brother. Then, some years later, he had to go into battle once more against his uncle, Nayan, Prince of Manchuria, who had rebelled against him.

The battle against Nayan, Prince of Manchuria

When he heard that the Prince of Manchuria was riding with his war host to attack him, Khubilai Khan secretly called together an army of 360,000 horsemen and 100,000 foot soldiers, taking them only from his personal retinue so that the news would not get about.

Then, sitting in a wooden turret mounted on four elephants, Khubilai Khan rode to Nayan's camp with his war host. Quickly his soldiers surrounded the enemy camp. The Mongols began to play their instruments and sing, and when the great copper drum boomed out the two armies fell on each other.

A savage battle was fought that day until Nayan's troops were put to flight. Nayan himself was taken prisoner and executed.

After the battle the Muslim and Buddhist soldiers in the Great Khan's army mocked the Christians who had been fighting for Nayan, who was himself a Christian. They said that obviously the Christian God had not been strong enough to help the defeated prince.

Then Khubilai Khan showed what a wise ruler he was. He called out to the Christians:

"Your God did not help the traitor Nayan because He is on the side of justice and right."

This made the Christian soldiers feel that they would not be wrong to obey Khubilai Khan, and also that he respected their religion.

Then the great Mongol emperor, Khubilai Khan, returned to the capital of his empire in Peking, where surrounded by pomp and splendor, he ordered a great feast to celebrate the victory.

Khubilai Khan rode to Nayan's camp with his war host

Peking

The Great Khan was a merciful emperor, anxious to avoid bloodshed whenever possible. At his court he kept magicians who he thought could help him avert disasters and it was because of them that the ancient city of Peking was rebuilt.

One day soothsayers came to the Great Khan and warned him that the inhabitants of the ancient city of Peking were destined to revolt against him. Khubilai Khan believed them and decided that if they were made the inhabitants of another town this omen would not come true. So he ordered a new city to be built beside the old one and moved all the inhabitants into it. Of course he could have had all the people put to death instead. This is probably what his ancestor Genghis Khan would have done. But Khubilai Khan loved his people. He did not believe in killing unless it was absolutely necessary.

The new city was surrounded by high white walls. Each wall had three gates let into it and roads, straight as arrows, stretched across the city from each gate.

A fine bell tower stood in the center of Peking. Every evening the bell rang out three times. This was the signal for all the gates to be closed. From that moment nobody was allowed to leave the city except in a case of great emergency.

The Great Khan's palace joined onto the city wall. It was, said Marco Polo, the largest palace that had ever been seen. It consisted of many halls and pavilions, gardens and courtyards, all designed by the most skillful Chinese architects. The lacquered roofs glittered in all the colors of the rainbow. Their radiance could be seen from far away.

The walls of every room were covered with beaten gold and decorated with pictures of ladies and horsemen, birds and animals. The throne room was so vast that there was room for six thousand people in it.

In his park, north of the palace, the Great Khan had ordered a great mound to be raised. It was planted all over with evergreen trees and the ground was paved with lapis lazuli, so that everything reflected a beautiful blue-green light.

On top of this mound stood the palace of the Great Khan's grandson who was to be his heir. His name was Temur. He was the son of Khubilai Khan's eldest son Chinghiz, who unfortunately had died young.

The Great Khan spent three months of every year—December, January and February—in his great palace at Peking.

His four wives lived here. Each was an empress and had a special court of her own.

His Imperial Guard consisted of twelve thousand horsemen. They were divided into four companies, each company being on duty for three days at a time.

The Great Khan's feasts

When he gave a feast the Great Khan's table stood at the northern end of the great hall on a dais. Next to him sat his favorite wife. On his right, and a little below him, were the tables of his sons and other royal kinsmen. Lower down sat the court officials, the nobles and their wives. Then came the soldiers.

On a table near the Great Khan stood a large golden vessel filled with wine. On either side stood two smaller vessels containing other drinks. Everybody drank out of gold cups and the servants saw to it that the cups were never empty.

Special servants attended the Great Khan. They kept their mouths and noses covered with silk cloths so that their breath could not touch the food they gave him.

Whenever the Great Khan raised his cup to drink, all the instruments played a fanfare and the guests fell on their knees, remaining in this position until he had finished drinking.

At the end of the feast a great troupe of acrobats would come into the hall to entertain the guests.

The Great Khan's soldiers wore large gold belts and boots of chamois leather embroidered with silver thread

The two most important feasts of the year took place on September 28th which was the Great Khan's birthday, and at New Year, which under the Mongols fell the first week in February. Both were celebrated with great pomp.

On the Great Khan's birthday everybody wore suits made of cloth of gold decorated with pearls and precious stones. Even the soldiers wore special clothes with large gold belts, and boots of chamois leather embroidered with silver thread. It was proclaimed a holiday throughout the Great Khan's lands and every province in his realm sent him a costly present.

As soon as an animal broke cover, the men would loose the dogs

The feast at New Year was called the White Festival. On this day everybody wore white clothes for good luck, and although the gifts sent to the Great Khan were made of gold, silver and precious stones, they were designed so that the chief color of each was white too. This festival ended in a grand procession of the Great Khan's ten thousand white horses and five thousand elephants. They passed before him covered in silk draperies, embroidered with gold, bearing boxes filled with gold plate and other precious objects. It was a dazzling and awe-inspiring sight. No wonder Marco Polo thought Khubilai Khan the most splendid ruler in the world.

The Great Khan's hunting parties

One of the things Khubilai Khan loved doing most of all was hunting. Wherever he lived he was always ready to ride out with his many different trained animals to hunt in the surrounding countryside. Xanadu was his favorite hunting palace, but even when he was in Peking he only had to ride for two or three days to reach a plain where there were many animals for him to kill.

After his three months' stay in Peking he would set out in March and travel

south towards the sea. He would take with him a large pack of hounds and mastiffs who were in the charge of two brothers called Bayan and Mingan. In addition to the dogs, each brother had ten thousand men under his command.

When they reached a district rich in game, Bayan with his ten thousand men would stand in a line to the left of the Great Khan, and Mingan with his men would stand in a line to his right. Then they would move forward across the country, driving the game before them. As soon as an animal broke cover, the men would loose the dogs.

When he hunted larger animals like buffalo, bears or wild boars, the Great Khan used leopards, and even tigers, which were taken to the hunting ground in cages, for they were too ferocious to be taken with the party in any other way.

Sometimes, particularly as he grew older, the Great Khan preferred falconry to other more strenuous forms of hunting. On these occasions he would ride in a beautiful litter carried on the backs of four elephants. His friends rode along by his side, keeping him company and talking to him. Whenever they saw a flock of cranes flying towards them they would warn the Great Khan so that he could open the roof of his litter and loose his falcons.

Then, when they reached the sea, they would set up camp. Here they would stay until Easter, hunting the cranes, swans and other birds.

Many years later, when he was back in Venice again, Marco Polo described Khubilai Khan's feasts and hunting expeditions in great detail. He had a first-hand knowledge of them, for Khubilai Khan was interested in Marco. He kept Marco near him and, beside hunting and feasting, also gave Marco the opportunity of listening to the conversations of some of the most gifted and civilized men in the Eastern world.

It was a pity that Marco was not better educated himself. Nearly everything he heard discussed—about poetry, philosophy or religion, for example—was above his head. But he kept his eyes open—very sharp eyes they were, too—and relied on his experience as a merchant's son when it came to valuing the things he saw and deciding what use they might be either to the Great Khan or, later, to merchants who wanted to trade with the East.

The Great Khan's money

One of the things that astonished him most was the use of paper for money in the Great Khan's realms instead of the gold and silver coins which were used everywhere else. As a matter of fact Khubilai Khan was the first person ever to think of using paper money.

Marco Polo described how the paper was made out of the bark of a mulberry tree and cut up into various sizes to represent different values. Each piece was stamped with the Great Khan's own seal. He could hardly believe his eyes when he saw the merchants give valuable goods like pearls, gems and gold in exchange for this paper, which seemed quite worthless to him.

What is more, a proclamation was sent, from time to time, to every town in the Great Khan's empire, ordering all stocks of gold and silver and precious stones to be brought to the Great Khan's mint in Peking. And to Marco Polo's surprise the governors of the towns obeyed this order and promptly sent such enormous wagon-loads of treasure that, when Marco Polo saw them, he said it was beyond any man's power to guess how much there was. When the treasure arrived at the mint it was weighed out and the value paid over to the governors of the towns in paper money. And nobody seemed to think this a bad exchange.

Marco Polo supposed that the merchants and the town governors only accepted the paper money because the Great Khan had commanded them to do so. He did not understand at all that each piece of paper represented a part of the Great Khan's treasure in much the same way that modern bank notes represent the gold reserves of the country in which they are issued.

The Great Khan's communications

Another interesting sight was the system of communications which the Great Khan had organized to link up the different parts of his empire. Roads were built from Peking to all the different towns and countries, and along these roads the Great Khan's foot messengers and mounted messengers hurried by day and night to pass on the Great Khan's commands.

The foot messengers wore great belts set with bells which rang loudly as they ran, warning the posting station down the road that a messenger was on his way. The messenger would run as hard as he could for three miles to the next posting station. Here a fresh messenger would take over the message and run on to the next station. In this way a ten days' journey could be covered in just one day and one night.

The mounted messengers also had their posting stations along the main roads. They were set at intervals of twenty-five miles and were supplied with every comfort. The mounted messengers could travel a distance of two hundred and even three hundred miles in one day, by using very much the same system as the foot messengers.

By means of his messengers the Great Khan could keep informed of everything that was happening in his empire. He would be told at once if there was famine in any district or when some sudden disaster had occurred. It was because the Great Khan was so anxious that no harm should come to his people that he had set up this swift system of messengers, said Marco Polo. For the instant he heard of a disaster, he was busy sending money or animals to the stricken area. Truly, Khubilai Khan was the greatest emperor in the world.

MARCO POLO TRAVELS AS THE GREAT KHAN'S COMMISSIONER

As soon as he had arrived at the Great Khan's court, Marco Polo set to work. He learned to speak and write the Mongol language perfectly. Then he studied some of the other languages which were spoken by the foreign officials in the Great Khan's government. Nobody now knows what these were, but they probably included Arabic, Tibetan and Chinese.

When Khubilai Khan noticed that Marco was eager to learn all he could, he began to take an interest in him. He saw that Marco was quick to observe what went on around him. He was discreet, too, and careful not to offend the other courtiers. As time went on the Great Khan decided that Marco would be a very useful man to have in his service and, after the young Venetian had been at court for about two years, the Great Khan made him a commissioner. Then he sent him on several tours of inspection to the different countries in his empire.

Marco Polo's job was to find out how the local governments looked after the people in their charge, to see how the money was spent which was taken from the people in the form of taxes, and generally to report on anything which might be useful for the Great Khan to know, whether it had to do with government matters or not.

During his tours of inspection Marco Polo was able to travel in comfort through parts of Asia which nobody in Europe even knew existed. It gave the young man from Venice a wonderful chance to gather practical information about the people who lived there and the sort of goods they had to sell.

The first journey he made for the Great Khan was to those parts of Asia which are now known as Burma and Indochina. The map at the beginning of the book shows which way he went.

One day the pages threatened to kill the king if he did not come to the court of their master, Prester John

Prester John ordered the Golden King to be brought into his presence

Marco Polo's journey to Burma and Indochina

With a large company of attendants, Marco left Peking and traveled south for ten miles until he reached the River Hun-ho. An immense marble bridge stretched across the river. It was built on twenty-four arches and piers. Marble columns, each supporting a carved lion, were set along the parapet on both sides of the bridge. Marco Polo was impressed by its size and said it was the finest bridge in the world.

After crossing the river the company of horsemen rode to Cho-chau, a town which Marco noted was famous for its embroidered fabrics.

Then the road led through the silk manufacturing town of T'ai-yuan-fu to Caichu. Here there was a castle which had been built by a ruler, known as the Golden King, who had reigned over this land in the time of Prester John. Marco Polo was told the following story about him.

Prester John had been at war with the Golden King for many years, but the castle was so strongly fortified that he could never get the better of him. This annoyed Prester John very much.

One day seven faithful pages came to Prester John. Humbly, they fell on their knees before him.

"Lord, if it be your will, we shall bring the Golden King to you," they said.

Prester John at once gave them leave to try.

Then the seven pages rode off to the Golden King's castle at Caichu. When they arrived there they begged to be taken into his service. The Golden King was flattered to think the servants of Prester John should prefer to work for him. He agreed gladly. For two years they attended the Golden King faithfully and he came to love them as if they had been his children.

But the seven pages had only been waiting for a chance to catch him off his guard. One day when the king was out riding with them they laid hands on their swords and threatened to kill him instantly if he did not come to the court of their master, Prester John.

The Golden King was so full of grief because of their betrayal that he allowed himself to be brought before Prester John. He was stripped of his royal clothes and forced to work as a herdsman, one of the humblest servants of Prester John's household.

After he had spent two years doing this lowly work, he was once more brought into Prester John's presence. Prester John ordered his servants to dress him in splendid robes. Then he greeted the Golden King as a royal person and said:

"Golden King, do you now see that you are not powerful enough to fight against me?"

"It is true," replied the Golden King.

"In that case I shall distress you no further," declared Prester John. "Return to your kingdom and in future, remember that you are my faithful vassal and offend me no more."

Then, loading him with many rich gifts, Prester John gave the Golden King his freedom. The Golden King kept his word and from that time on there was always friendship between them.

After they had passed the Golden King's castle, the horsemen rode west until they came to the River Hwang-ho, which means "Yellow" River. Then, still further west, they came to the city of Si-ngan-fu, which was ruled by one of the Great Khan's sons whose name was Mangalai.

Marco Polo visited the beautiful palace in which he lived. It lay in the plain down by the river amid gardens and fountains. Like most Eastern royal palaces it was enormous and richly decorated with beaten gold. As a result of his visit, Marco was able to report that Mangalai was a good and just governor, well loved by his subjects.

So far, his journey had taken him through the most densely populated and wealthy provinces of the Great

The travelers cut down bamboo canes

Khan's realm. But after he left Mangalai's palace at Si-ngan-fu, Marco Polo's road led through the mountainous province of Hanchung. Here the country was poor and there were hardly any inhabitants: the few they saw were primitive farmers and hunters. Although there was probably no danger, for only the most desperate bandits would have attacked such a large company, Marco Polo must have been relieved to reach the city of Ch'êng-tu-fu after traveling through such dismal regions for twenty days.

Ch'êng-tu-fu lay on the banks of a tributary of the River Yang-tze-Kiang or Blue River. It was the chief city of southern China. It had once been the capital city of an emperor and was still a very important trade center. In his account Marco Polo said that it was hard to count the ships which traveled up and down the river bringing all kinds of rich merchandise to the town.

The bridge over the river was made of marble. It was covered by a roof supported on marble columns. It must have been very wide, for Marco said that wooden booths were set up there every day and that it was used as a market-place.

After leaving Ch'êng-tu-fu, Marco Polo traveled on into southern Tibet. His road led through the bamboo forests at the foot of the great mountains so he only saw a small part of that country. But what he did see was desolate and in ruins as a result of Mongu Khan's invasion, some years before.

While he was traveling through the bamboo forests a fire broke out. The heat and the flames caused the bamboo canes to explode with such loud cracking sounds that Marco was terrified until he found out what was causing the noise. The horses, too, nearly went mad with fear and would have bolted if they had not been tied up.

When they had got used to it, however, the noise of these exploding bamboos could be turned to good advantage. The forests teemed with savage animals, and since they were as frightened of the noise as Marco had been the travelers cut down bamboo canes and used them for firewood on their campfires at night.

They often had to camp by the road at night, for there were no towns and few villages here. Further on, however, they came to a more settled area, but the people in these parts were poor. They dressed in skins or rags. "Moreover," said Marco, deeply impressed, "some of them are extremely skilled in magic arts and perform such marvelous and diabolic feats that nobody would believe me if I described them."

Days passed into weeks as they slowly traveled on towards Burma, keeping their eyes open for interesting things to tell the Great Khan.

They came to a lake where people fished for pearls, and a mountain from which the precious stone turquoise could be mined. Marco noted down these places as being of interest to merchants —and also the fact that the people here liked to be paid in salt.

Then they rejoined the Yang-tze-Kiang River, further down its course this time. Across the river lay the frontier of a province called Yünnan.

In Yünnan gold could be found in most of the lakes as well as in the mountains. The people used sea-shells for money in this place. And it was here that, for the first time in his life, Marco came across crocodiles.

"A great serpent lives here," Marco wrote. "It is a dreadful beast ten paces long and ten palms wide. It has two legs armed with claws in front near its head and its head and jaw are so immensely large that it can swallow a man in one mouthful. By day these animals remain underground because of the great heat, but at night they come out to hunt for food and to drink at the river."

From this description it is clear that Marco Polo did not really go close enough to see one properly, for a crocodile has four legs, not two, and it does not live under-

The huntsmen trapped crocodiles by driving stakes into the ground

Merchants came from far away to buy and sell gold and silver

ground. It spends most of the day in the water, only coming on land at nightfall.

He was told that the huntsmen trapped the crocodiles by driving stakes into the ground and then covering them with sand. Coming on land at night the crocodile would be pierced by these stakes and die at once. The gall bladder of the dead crocodile was used by local doctors to cure anybody who had been bitten by a mad dog.

Five days west of Yünnan lay the province of Zar-dandan. Marco Polo found a lot to write down about the people who lived here. To begin with, their religion was quite unlike any religion he had come across before. They worshiped their ancestors. Then, some of their customs were very strange.

The men covered their teeth with gold and went to bed for forty days every time their wives had a baby, as if they had brought the child into the world themselves. None of the people could write. Instead, when they wanted to keep a record of payments they cut notches in a piece of wood.

Perhaps the strangest thing of all was the way in which they cured a sick man.

At the first sign of illness, sorcerers were sent for. They examined the patient to discover his symptoms. Then they began to sing and dance, keeping this up until one of them fell to the ground unconscious. At this point the others would question him.

"What is wrong with him?" they would ask. And "Why is he suffering?"

Then the apparently unconscious sorcerer would reply:

"He is ill because he has offended a certain spirit."

At once the other sorcerers would start chanting.

"Spirit, ah spirit, please forgive this man. If you do, he will give you whatever you wish."

If the sick man was very ill and looked as if he would die, the sorcerer would say that the spirit could never forgive him. But if he looked as if he might recover, he would tell the other sorcerers what sacrifice the spirit would accept in order to forgive the sick man.

The sacrifices were usually a certain number of black-headed sheep and expensive drinks. The blood of the dead sheep would be sprinkled all over the house. Then the meat would be cooked and the drinks prepared. While this was being done the sorcerers went on dancing and singing. They would also run through the house from top to bottom, burning incense and myrrh and setting up lights wherever they went.

Specially skilled people hunted the lions with a trained dog

Just before the food was ready to be eaten they would again ask whether the sick man had been forgiven. If the reply was yes, they would all have a great feast and return peacefully to their homes. Marco was told that this treatment always worked and that the sick man got well at once.

After they had passed through this province, Marco and his companions had nearly reached the first place they were making for. They only had to climb down through the mountains past a famous market place, where merchants from all over the country came to buy and sell their stores of gold and silver. Then they reached Burma.

Burma was a country of dense jungles. The forests were full of wild elephants, said Marco Polo, and unicorns too. In those days people believed there was an animal, half horse and half deer, which had a slender, twisted horn on its forehead. They called it the unicorn. But nobody had ever seen a unicorn, so probably when Marco Polo saw a one-horned rhinoceros he thought it was the legendary creature. Beyond the jungle lay the capital city of Burma called Tagaung.

In Tagaung there was a famous tomb in which an ancient king lay buried. Above the king's grave two enormous towers rose into the air, one plated with gold and the other with silver. The top of each tower ended in a little cupola set with bells which rang merrily in the wind.

During the conquest of Tagaung, the Khan's soldiers wanted to pull down the tomb in order to send the gold and silver on the towers to the Great Khan. But he ordered them not to touch it because he knew that the dead king had built this tomb for the peace of his soul.

When Marco had finished his work in Burma, he rode north until he came to the country of Laos. Here there were more strange customs to record, for the people tattooed themselves all over with strange designs of birds and animals, considering most handsome the person who had the most tattoo marks on his body.

Astrologers prophesied the fall of his empire

After Laos, they journeyed through North Vietnam. The inhabitants of this region were more primitive. Here they were brown-skinned and warlike. Both men and women were fond of wearing gold or silver bracelets on their arms and legs.

They now traveled along the banks of a large river, passing through a dangerous region full of lions. "There were so many lions," wrote Marco Polo, "that nobody dares to go out of doors after nightfall." But he went on to say that there were specially skilled people who hunted the lions with trained dogs. The dogs were so clever that two of them working together could track down a lion and be certain of killing it.

Marco Polo had made quite

a considerable detour, traveling north from Burma through Indo-china. Now that he had visited all the regions about which the Great Khan wanted information, he continued north-west in order to reach Ch'êng-tu-fu again. From here, he returned to Peking along the road he had taken on his outward journey. And so he completed his first mission.

Bayan with the hundred eyes conquered the empire

Marco Polo's travels in the eastern regions of China

During the course of his work as a commissioner, Marco Polo had to make many journeys to the cities on the east coast of China. This region was the richest and most civilized in the whole world. A Chinese dynasty of emperors, whose family name was Sung, had ruled here for thousands of years without being worried much by invaders. Then, in 1273, soon after Marco had arrived at the Great Khan's court, the Mongol armies invaded the empire and conquered it.

At that time the emperor was only two years old and the country was being ruled for him by his mother.

The Mongol armies found it very easy to take over the country. The people were not at all warlike. They spent the time enjoying themselves in their own very civilized way. They liked painting, reading and discussing new ideas. In order to be able to live like this they had to have peace and quiet. And instead of keeping a powerful army to discourage other people from attacking them, they relied on an old prophecy which astrologers had made to an emperor called Facfur, long since dead. The astrologers told Facfur that the empire would not fall until a man with a hundred eyes came to take it. This made them feel very safe, for who had ever heard of a man with a hundred eyes?

Now it so happened that the Mongol armies were commanded by a general called Bayan Chincsan. When the mother of the baby emperor heard about him she did not try to defend the country. She surrendered at once. For in the Chinese language the name "Bayan Chincsan" could mean "Bayan with the hundred eyes" and she believed that the old prophecy had now come true.

It was lucky for her, and for the inhabitants of the empire, that it was Khubilai Khan's Mongols and not those of Genghis Khan who had invaded the country. Instead of killing the imperial family and sacking the town, Bayan treated the empress with great respect. He sent her and the baby emperor to the court of the Great Khan where they were looked after by one of Khubilai's four empresses. Then he took over the government and let the people lead their old peaceful lives.

When he visited these regions, Marco Polo's keen eye for outward appearances took note of the wealth and luxury he saw wherever he went. He was a practical man, quick to notice where the money came from, how the trade in various goods was carried out, but to the Chinese people he must have seemed even less civilized than the Mongol invaders. Nowhere in his book does Marco Polo comment on the great tradition of poetry, sculpture and pottery for which this dynasty was to become so famous. He did not have the education to understand, let alone appreciate, what he saw. All it meant to him was that the people were rich rather than poor, and placid instead of warlike.

He admired their buildings, he was surprised by some of the details of their way of life—how many baths they took, what sort of clothes they wore, the food they ate—and he was impressed by the efficient way in which they ran such public services as the police and the fire departments.

Here are some of the cities which Marco Polo described.

He noted that Hwai-ngan-chau, the first city across the frontier, was a prosperous trading center.

Further south lay Yang-chau. The Great Khan appointed Marco Polo governor of this town and he ruled it for three years.

A little to the west lay a powerful city called Siang-yang-fu. This town was able to hold out against the invaders for three years. Although the Mongol armies laid siege to the town the inhabitants did not starve, for they were able to get food from a lake which lay to the south of the city.

While this was going on, Niccolo, Maffeo, and Marco were at the Great Khan's

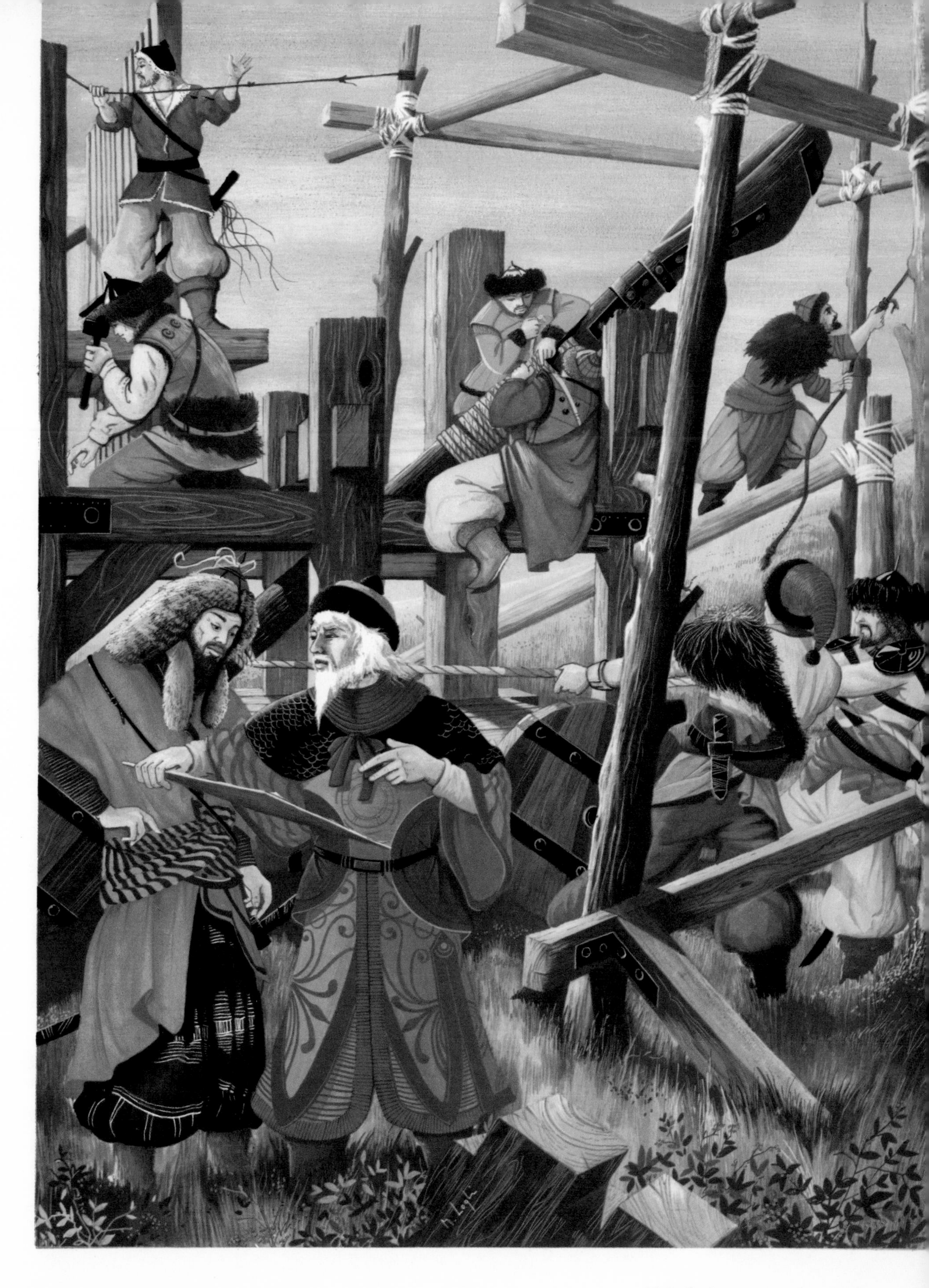

He built three enormous catapults

court in Peking. When they heard about the siege and learned that the Mongol armies were on the point of giving up their attempt to take the city they went to the Great Khan with a suggestion. They told him that one of the people who had traveled from Europe with them was a skilled craftsman who could make such powerful engines of war that no city would be able to hold out against them.

The Great Khan listened to what they had to say. Then he gave orders for the man to be sent out to the besieging army. As soon as he had arrived there he built three enormous catapults, each of which was able to hurl heavy stones weighing three hundred pounds.

Catapults were one of the most important weapons an army could use against a fortress before gunpowder and cannons were invented. To build and fire them needed great skill. They could cause heavy damage, even though they were not very accurate and took a long time to load.

When the inhabitants of the city saw their houses being destroyed by these heavy stones they were so frightened that they surrendered at once.

On the river Yangtse Kiang lay another prosperous trading city called Sinju. It had a good harbor in which a large fleet of merchant ships could lie anchored at once.

The Yangtse Kiang is a very broad river. At several points it is more than ten miles wide. Marco Polo reported that more goods were carried on its waters than on all the rivers in the Christian world and the Mediterranean put together. "I can assure you," he wrote, "that I saw five thousand ships in this city at once and it is by no means a large city. Just imagine, then, how many ships there must be in the other cities along the river, for there are two hundred of them and all much larger than this one."

East of Sinju lay Chin-Kiang-fu, ruled by a Christian governor whom the Great Khan had appointed. Near by lay the ruined city of Chang-chau.

When the Mongol armies invaded Chang-chau, the soldiers seized the local wine. It was so delicious that they drank all they could find and, in the end, fell down in a deep sleep wherever they happened to be. When the inhabitants of the town saw their enemies asleep in the streets they killed them all and not one man escaped. Even so, it was not long before Bayan with the hundred eyes heard what had happened. At once he sent a strong force which razed the city to the ground and put all the inhabitants to the sword.

South of Chang-chau lay another great town called Su-chau. Marco Polo described it as being forty miles around and inhabited by countless people. There were six thousand stone bridges in this town and they were so high that a fully rigged galley could pass under them.

A man was stationed at the top of a tall tower, ready to give the alarm if fire should break out

The great city of Hang-chau

Three days' journey from Su-chau lay the great city of Hang-chau, which means "City of Heaven" in Chinese. This was the capital city of what had been the Sung Empire and it was more beautiful and imposing, thought Marco, than any other town in the world.

Marco Polo methodically listed the things he noticed. First of all its size, which Marco said was more than a hundred miles around. This shows how impressed he

"The men of Fu-chau are the most savage people in the world . . ."

was. In fact he must have exaggerated. Nevertheless the city was divided into one hundred and sixty districts called toumans. Each touman represented ten thousand houses. The names of the people living in each house were written on the door. The same was true of the inns, even the names of visitors and the day they arrived being written up, so that at any time, the governor and his administrators could know who was living in the city.

The city was surrounded by water and crossed by hundreds of canals. Marco Polo counted twelve thousand stone bridges in the city alone. Each of these bridges was guarded night and day by a troop of ten men, who were there to prevent robberies.

This is what Marco had to say about the work done by the people:

"The inhabitants follow twelve different arts or professions, each of which has two thousand workshops, each giving employment to from ten to forty men. By law everyone must work at the craft which his father followed and nobody may take up a different calling however profitable it might be for him.

"The shops are without number. And as for the nobility, they do not do any work with their hands. The men live royally and the women hardly go out at all, being served in everything as if they were angels."

There were many stone towers with thick walls placed all over the town. When

fire broke out, the inhabitants could carry their property into these towers for safety. Since most of the houses were made of wood there were a great many fires, and these towers were very necessary.

There was another fire precaution too. On a hill in the center of the town a tall tower had been built. A man was constantly on guard there, ready to give the alarm if a fire should break out. When he saw any suspicious signs he would immediately beat a heavy gong. The sound of this gong could be heard for miles.

Then there were the baths. Marco Polo counted three thousand hot bath establishments, some of them so large that a hundred people could get into a bath at one time. He said the people were very fond of cleanliness and would take a bath every day, besides washing before meals.

The palace of the deposed emperor was surrounded by gardens, lakes and orchards. It contained a magnificent hall decorated in blue and gold and painted with scenes from history. The roof was of pure gold.

A large lake lay outside the city. It was thirty miles around and on its shores were splendid palaces and Buddhist monasteries. In the middle of the lake there were two islands, on each of which stood a pavilion, "so elegantly constructed that it might be the palace of a king."

These pavilions were used for picnics, banquets and wedding feasts.

The men of Fu-chau decorated their faces with blue designs

Hang-chau lay on a river only fifteen miles from the seaport of Kan-pu. Ships from all over the world called in at Kan-pu to discharge their cargoes and take on board fresh merchandise.

The Kingdom of Fu-chau

After spending some time in Hang-chau, enjoying the delights and luxuries of that city, it must have been very unpleasant for Marco to leave it and travel south to the kingdom of Fu-chau, for the people here were as different as they could be from the peace-loving, industrious inhabitants of Cathay. Marco Polo's description of them is horrifying.

"The men of this region eat the flesh of animals which would be repugnant to us and even human flesh, which is considered very good. When they go to war, they cut their hair, leaving only a tuft on the top of the scalp and they decorate their faces with blue designs, laid on with the tip of a lance. They are the most savage men in all the lands of the Chinese and the most cruel in the world. They do nothing but fight and kill, drinking the blood of their dead enemies and eating their bodies afterwards. They gain nothing else by their own labors."

Nevertheless he was able to report that this was a rich spice-growing country and that there was a large city on the banks of a river, called Kien-ning-fu, which did a thriving trade in precious stones.

South of Fu-chau lay the seaport of Zaiton. Ships from India landed their goods here, the Great Khan receiving a ten per cent customs duty.

While he was in eastern China, Marco was told about a fabulous country called Japan.

JAPAN AND INDIA

Marco Polo never visited Japan himself, but he tried to find out as much as he could about it. For one thing nobody in Europe had any idea that such a large, rich island even existed. For another, the inhabitants had been strong enough to defeat the Mongol armies when they invaded Japan in 1281.

Marco Polo described it as the largest of many islands lying some 1,500 miles east of China in the China Sea. The inhabitants were fair-skinned; they were handsome and had beautiful manners. They were ruled by an emperor who lived in a splendid palace with a roof made entirely of gold. Apart from the gold which it was thought could be found all over Japan in enormous quantities, the island was also immensely rich in pearls and precious stones.

When travelers told Khubilai Khan how wealthy the island was, he decided to conquer it. He sent two of his generals, called Abakan and Vonsamchin, to the island with a great fleet of ships and soldiers.

The two generals landed on the island at the head of a powerful army, but before they had time to occupy a single town a terrible cyclone blew up. At once the soldiers took to their boats again and put out to sea. But the cyclone grew ever more fierce and a great part of the fleet was shipwrecked. Those soldiers who were not drowned managed to struggle to a neighboring island and there they stayed, for the men in the boats which had not been wrecked abandoned their comrades and sailed for home.

When the storm died down it was soon clear to the Japanese that the survivors on the island, who numbered some 30,000, were helpless. Pleased to think that the Mongols were now at their mercy, they set off in their own ships to capture

The people of Japan worshiped idols

the enemy soldiers. As soon as they came to the island, the Japanese soldiers leaped ashore and streamed inland after the Mongols, leaving their ships unguarded. The Mongols saw this and took heart. They lured the Japanese soldiers to follow them on a detour and, coming on the abandoned ships from another direction, boarded them and sailed across to Japan.

Then, having landed, they hoisted the Japanese standards which they found on the ships, and marched on the capital. Seeing the standards the inhabitants mistook the soldiers for their own people and did nothing to stop them, so that they were able to take the town quite easily.

When they realized what had happened, the Japanese were furious. They laid siege to the city and guarded it so closely that not one Mongol messenger could get through to the Great Khan with a message asking for help. In the end, it was only by a remarkably clever piece of bargaining that the Mongols were able to surrender to the Japanese on condition that their lives were spared.

When he heard what had happened the Great Khan was very angry about the inefficient way in which the campaign had been conducted. He arrested the generals and had them put to death.

The people of Japan worshiped many different idols, some with the heads of rams, some with those of bulls or pigs. Marco mentioned this in his book and also the rumor that they ate their captured enemies, but this statement was, in fact, untrue, for the Japanese were a highly civilized people.

Marco Polo got all his information about Japan from other people who said they had been there. Some of it was accurate but some was quite untrue. Since he had no way of checking it, Marco simply wrote down everything he was told.

The Indies

Marco Polo called all the country between China and Africa the "Indies." This is because Hindu colonizers had, many centuries before, brought their civilization to the lands between Burma and China. The powerful Hindu kingdoms which had grown up were as rich in beautiful sculptures and architecture as India itself, but when Marco Polo visited them they were starting to decline. Not long after he had been there they fell into ruin and the jungle covered up all trace of them.

Marco Polo, traveling through these lands, ignored the signs of a wealthy civilization originating from India and kept his sharp eye open for the sort of facts which a merchant or a traveler might wish to know.

From Zaiton he sailed south-west for one thousand five hundred miles to the Hindu kingdom, which was called Chamba. This country paid an annual tribute of twenty elephants to the Great Khan and was famous for its aloe wood and ebony.

In Basman there was a small kind of rhinoceros

The next place he described was the large island called Java, to which many merchants came for its spices and other riches. In those days it was thought to be the largest island in the world. It had not been conquered by the Great Khan, however, for it lay too far away.

To the west, the Malay Peninsula was wild and uninhabited, though Marco heard that there was plenty of gold to be found there. Singapore, a little further to the east, was then a wilderness overgrown with thickets and aromatic trees.

The island of Lesser Java (now Sumatra), which he visited next, was divided into a number of kingdoms. The first, Ferlec, had been visited so often by trading Saracens that most of the inhabitants living on the coast had been converted to the Muslim religion. The people who lived inland in the mountains were very savage, however, and ate human flesh.

The people of the second kingdom, Basman, were very savage too, according to Marco Polo. Here there were elephants and a small kind of rhinoceros.

In those days European people still believed in the legendary unicorn. Now Marco was able to note down that the unicorn, far from being half deer, half horse, was a shaggy-haired animal only a little smaller than an elephant. "It has one black horn in the middle of its forehead. Some people say that this animal lets itself be caught by maidens but this is not true . . ." he wrote.

Another myth he exploded was the one about the tiny people of Basman, mummies of which had been shipped to Europe by Eastern traders. People had been marveling for a long time about the tiny, perfectly formed men who must live in this land, and now Marco Polo was able to see with his own eyes that they were really monkeys which had been treated to remove the hair from their bodies in order to make them look like men.

The next kingdom was called Sumatra. Marco Polo was forced to stay here for five months because of the monsoon storms. While he was there he saw people extract "wine" from a kind of palm tree. They would make a cut in the bark and tie a pot under the cut to catch the liquid which ran out. He was very impressed by this remarkable plant which he was also to find in many of the other Eastern countries through which he traveled.

In Dagroian, the next country, he encountered a rather horrible custom. When a man was dangerously ill, the sorcerers would be called in. If they decided that the man was too ill to recover he would at once be put to death. Then his body was cooked and eaten by his sorrowing relatives. The bones would be carefully collected and put in a casket which was then set in a cave in the mountains where they would be safe from wild animals.

The fifth kingdom was called Lambri. Here Marco found groves of spice trees—camphor, brazil and many others. He brought a shoot of a brazil tree back to Venice with him but the climate was too cold for it and it did not survive.

In Lambri he was amazed to see what he took to be men with long tails. Actually they were monkeys, which lived in the mountains, and were too shy to come close enough to be recognized.

The last of the kingdoms on the island of Lesser Java was called Fansur. Here again there was plenty of camphor, and as grain would not grow there the inhabitants ate rice instead. Marco Polo mentioned that as well as drawing wine from trees, the inhabitants of this country could get flour from them too.

"There is, too, a great marvel in this place: a flour which is obtained from trees. In truth there are certain large trees which, under a covering of soft bark, have a layer of flour from which an excellent dough can be made. I myself ate this dough many times." He was referring to sago. Marco Polo was the first European ever to eat sago.

When the monsoon storms were over, Marco Polo set sail again and traveled north of Lesser Java, passing two groups of islands, the Nicobar and Andaman Islands where a primitive race of people lived, quite untouched by any civilizing influence. Marco Polo found both their appearance and their customs horrible.

"The inhabitants," he wrote, "have no king. They live like beasts and wear no clothes at all. . . . The people (in the Andamans) have heads like dogs and their eyes are like those of a large mastiff. They have cruel natures and devour every man they can capture except for those of their own religion."

He noticed, nevertheless, that they raised cattle and rice crops.

Leaving these islands behind him, Marco Polo sailed south-west to Ceylon.

He described Ceylon as being a large island, two thousand four hundred miles round. On studying the charts made by local sailors, however, he discovered that the island had once been over a thou-

The fishermen would dive to a depth of six fathoms

sand miles larger and supposed that the strong north wind had brought in the sea to cover much of the land.

The inhabitants he encountered wore only a loincloth. They grew rice crops and made oil from the sesame seed. Their food was rice, milk and meat; and here, too, could be found the wine-bearing palm tree which he had seen in Sumatra.

The wife used to throw herself on her husband's funeral pyre

The chief importance of the island, so far as Marco Polo was concerned, was that precious stones could be found there. Sapphires, topazes, amethysts, and above all, rubies were there in large quantities. The king, who was called Sendeman, owned an enormous ruby. It was as red as fire and without a single flaw. It is thought that Marco had come to Ceylon to buy the ruby for the Great Khan, but the king would not part with it, for it was an heirloom in his family.

Marco was most contemptuous about the people who, he said, were a cowardly race. If there was any fighting to be done they called in soldiers from other regions, relying most heavily on the Saracens.

Coromandel, which lay sixty miles west of Ceylon on the coast of India proper, was the next stopping place. It was ruled by five kings, all brothers, the oldest of whom was called Sundara Pandi.

Marco gave details of a famous pearl fishery which existed here.

The pearls were gathered during the four weeks of April and the first two weeks of May. The fishermen would embark in large ships and sail out to sea for sixty miles. Then they would drop anchor.

The actual fishing was done from little boats which were lowered from the large ship. After rowing a little way out the fishermen would dive to a depth of six fathoms, cutting the pearl-bearing oysters from the sea-bed with their knives.

After each fishing trip the king would receive ten per cent of all the pearls which had been gathered, and the priests would receive five per cent in return for chanting prayers to the gods to preserve the fishermen from attack by sharks.

Marco added the curious information that the priests could only control the sharks by day and that was why nobody went pearl fishing after dark.

Here, too, the people wore only a loin-cloth and even the king did not wear more, but his was of specially beautiful cloth. He was immensely rich, too, for he never parted with any of his treasure and added to it constantly so that when he died he would have more to leave to his son than he himself had received from his father.

The king was served faithfully by his servants and friends throughout his life, and when he died they would throw themselves into the flames of his funeral pyre so that they could go on serving him in his next life.

Wives loved their husbands so much that they wanted to die with them rather than go on living by themselves, so they, too, used to throw themselves on the funeral pyre.

The eagles were forced to let go the meat

It was considered noble to take one's own life in such circumstances, and Marco Polo was told that criminals who had been condemned to death were given the chance to kill themselves in public in the name of one of their gods. If they decided to do this they were treated with great honor and respect.

Cattle were considered sacred, as they are to this day in India. Nobody was allowed to eat their flesh except the very lowliest people, and they could only do so after the animals had died a natural death.

Sacred dancers lived in the many Buddhist monasteries and temples. They were there to carry food to the idols and to entertain the images with singing and dancing.

Everybody kept an anxious eye open for omens, and a careful record was kept of the hour when each child was born and the planet under which the birth took place so that forecasts could be made of the sort of dangers and successes which might happen to them during their future lives.

"The people of Coromandel try to make themselves more dark-skinned than they already are," wrote Marco Polo. "They rub themselves with sesame oil, for they consider a dark skin very beautiful. That is why they paint their idols black and the images of their demons white. They have such faith in their oxen that they wear skirts of ox-skin as amulets when they go to war. As a result ox-skin is in great demand, for nobody feels safe if he does not carry some of it on his person."

Golconda, a thousand miles north of Coromandel, was ruled by a queen who was greatly loved by her people. This place was specially noticed by Marco Polo because of the many diamonds which could be found in the torrents and mountain crevasses. He described the rather ingenious method they had of extracting them from the deep ravines. People would go the mountains armed with pieces of meat which they would throw down the crevasses with such force that the diamonds lying at the bottom would stick to them. Then the eagles which lived in those mountains would swoop down after the meat and, carrying it up with them in their talons, would be forced by the people to let go the meat.

"But to return to the province of Coromandel . . ." wrote Marco Polo, who had learned that the body of a Christian saint lay buried there. And, collecting all the information he could, he wrote it down for the people in Europe, who would be especially interested in news of this kind.

The body of St. Thomas, the apostle, was said to lie buried in a little town. Few people lived there and no traders came to visit the place which was very out of the way. But both Christians and Saracens came to St. Thomas's tomb on pilgrimage. The Saracens who lived in Coromandel believed him to be a great Saracen prophet. They called him *avariun*, which means "holy man" in the Saracen language. The Christians also came to pray there and to take away a little of the red-colored earth from the place where the Saint died, for this was supposed to cure anyone who suffered from the ague, a malarial fever with hot and cold fits.

Marco Polo talked to the people who lived near the tomb. He asked them to tell him how St. Thomas had died. This was what they said had happened.

St. Thomas was praying in a lonely hermitage in the woods and round him stood many peacocks which were plentiful in that district. A poor man, who was hunting the peacocks, did not see St. Thomas. He shot an arrow and hit the apostle, who died quietly, still continuing his prayer.

The people also told Marco Polo about a miracle which had taken place a few years earlier.

A noble, who lived in the district, filled all the houses round the church with rice, using them as his storehouses, and so the pilgrims had nowhere to stay when they came to visit the tomb. The Christians who looked after the church were very angry about this and begged him to store his rice somewhere else. But he took no notice of them and would not clear the houses.

One night, St. Thomas appeared to him with a pitchfork in his hand. He held it at the noble's throat and said:

"If you do not take the rice out of my houses at once, you will come to a bad end." Then he pressed the pitchfork so hard against the noble's throat that the noble was in great pain. Then St. Thomas went away again.

The next morning the noble ordered the houses round the church to be cleared and told the Christians what had happened to him. They were overjoyed and were more proud of their saint than ever after that.

West of the place where St. Thomas lay buried was the province of Lar, from which, it was said, the Brahmans originally came. Marco was very impressed by these holy men. They were honest and faithful traders, he said, and never told a lie. They would not eat meat of any kind, because this would mean killing an animal and they regarded the taking of any life

One day, while he was out riding with his father, he saw the body of a dead man

as a dreadful sin. They would not drink alcohol either. And they could easily be distinguished from other people because they wore a cotton cord, which passed under their left shoulder and tied on their right.

They could discover omens in birds or other animals better than anyone else and they believed firmly in signs and omens. While they were discussing business matters they would watch their shadow and if it seemed larger or smaller than usual they would give up the trade they were discussing. Marco said they would even do so if they saw a tarantula spider coming towards them from an unfavorable direction.

"In Coilum there are black tigers, parrots and the most beautiful peacocks ever seen"

It was thought that the quiet, sober lives they led was the reason they lived to a very old age and in his book Marco wrote that the very holiest of them, who were called Yogi, lived to be as much as a hundred and fifty years old.

These Yogi went about completely naked, only rubbing a powder ground from ox bones into their skins. They lived on the dry leaves of banana trees, rice and milk, and once a month they would dose themselves with a medicine made of quicksilver, sulphur and water, which was said to prolong life.

There was a legend, which Marco Polo believed had grown up in Ceylon.

"There is in this island a mountain which is so steep that it can only be climbed by means of iron chains which hang down the sides," he wrote. "The Saracens say that on the summit is preserved the footprint of our first parent Adam, while the idolators [he meant Buddhists] maintain that it is the footprint of Sakyamuni or the Buddha, the first man who was worshiped as a god."

Sakyamuni was the son of a great and powerful king. When he was only a small child he dedicated himself to a life of prayer, for he had no interest in worldly things. This worried his father very much, for he had no other sons, and as Sakyamuni would have to become king one day he thought it was wrong for him to take so little interest in what went on around him. Besides, he did not understand that his son could be so different from all the other people and so he made Sakyamuni live in a splendid palace with gay companions who sang to him and danced before him and were there to keep all sad and painful thoughts away from him. He thought this would make the young prince learn to enjoy life. Sakyamuni spent many years in these luxurious surroundings but they did not change him one bit. He still went on praying and meditating just as if the palace, the gay companions and the singing and dancing did not exist at all.

The people of Ely were all pirates

Then, one day, two things happened which had a deep effect on him. He was out riding with his father when he saw the body of a dead man lying by the wayside. "What is that?" he asked, for he had never seen death before and did not know it existed. His father explained to him that all men must die and this made him very unhappy.

A little later on they passed a man who was so old that he had lost nearly all his teeth and could hardly walk. Now the young prince learned that men grow old, too.

When he returned to the palace he meditated about death and old age and became so unhappy that he could hardly bear it. He decided to go out into the world and look for the man who did not grow old and would never die. So he left the palace and traveled up into the high mountains. There he stayed for the rest of his life, passing every day in prayer and meditation.

When he died, his father was very unhappy. He ordered a golden statue to be made of the dead prince and ordered all the people in his kingdom to worship it as if it was a god.

This was the story Marco wrote in his book. "And it is said," he added, "that the prince lived eighty-four lives: the first as a man, the second as a bull, and the third as a horse, and so on, until at last he became a god. All the idolators worship this god and people come from far away on pilgrimage to this mountain in the island of Ceylon."

The Saracens, however, believed that it was the tomb of Adam and not of Sakyamuni. And when the Great Khan heard that Adam lay buried there, and that some teeth and a bowl had been found in the tomb, he was anxious to have these relics. So he sent ambassadors to Ceylon to ask for them. The King of Ceylon gave the relics to the Great Khan's ambassadors and they brought them to the Great Khan, who received them with great reverence.

After leaving Coromandel, Marco Polo traveled south to the city of Cail, which was ruled by Ashar, one of the five brother kings reigning over this region. The five brothers were always quarreling and there would often have been bitter war between them if their mother had not been there to keep the peace. All the same everybody felt very unsettled, for they knew that when she died there would be nobody to prevent the five kings from plunging the land into bloody wars.

South-west lay Coilum. "This country grows a great quantity of pepper and the climate is so hot that it would be possible for the people to boil eggs in the rivers . . ." wrote Marco Polo. And—"There are black tigers here and parrots and the most beautiful peacocks ever seen."

Then he went on to describe the inhabitants, who wore only a white loin cloth because of the heat and who made a very good wine out of the sugar which grew here.

Then came the savage region of Comorin and, three hundred miles to the north, Ely, where pepper, ginger and other spices could be found. There was no good port here, only a large river with a good estuary. There were few inhabitants apart from pirates who seized the goods of any ship which did not come there to trade.

"They say God sent you to us so that your goods should become ours," wrote Marco bitterly, "and they do not believe they have done any wrong. You will find the same thing all over the Indies."

Merchant ships called here every summer, but they had to load their cargoes in three or four days because it was unsafe to anchor on the sandy beaches.

Further north, Marco Polo visited the kingdom of Malabar—"a very large country, whose inhabitants do not have to pay tribute to anybody." They were ruled by a king and the chief religion was Buddhism.

The pirates would burn fires on the headlands in order to trap the merchant ships

Here again the coast was infested with pirates who used to put out to sea in large fleets carrying their wives and children with them. No ship which came within a hundred miles of the coast was safe, for the pirates would burn fires on the headlands in order to trap the merchant ships. However, they were only interested in loot and let the sailors go free.

There were more pirates in the kingdom of Thana, and here piracy was encouraged by the king, who let them keep all the goods they stole except for the horses.

"The gryphons here can lift an elephant into the air"

The islands of India

Marco Polo believed that Africa consisted of hundreds of islands. He called it "the islands of India." He had no idea that it was a continent. He had probably never been there himself and was only passing on the sort of information we would call "rumors."

The first two of these "islands" he heard were called "Male" and "Female" because all the men lived on the first and all the women and children on the second. The children were supposed to live with their mothers until they were fourteen years old. After that the sons went over to live with their fathers and the daughters remained with their mothers. The people were Christian and had a bishop. They were good fishermen and lived on rice, fish and milk.

The bishop, who looked after the Christians on these islands, was subject to the archbishop at Socotra, where the population was also Christian. Amber was the chief commodity found on that island and it provided a flourishing trade for the inhabitants.

The archbishop on Socotra was not subject to the Roman Pope, but to an archbishop who reigned from Baghdad.

Marco mentioned that the pirates came here to sell their loot and the people bought their goods because they had been told it had only been stolen from Saracens and Buddhists, not Christians.

Although the people were Christian they not only believed in sorcery but practiced magic arts, and the archbishop could not stop them. Rumors reached Marco Polo that their magic was so strong that they could call up contrary winds to send unwelcome ships away from their shores. "They can raise a storm at sea whenever they wish, change the direction of the wind as they desire and do many other marvelous things which are impossible for anyone to believe and so I shall not mention them," wrote Marco Polo.

In Madagascar there was a great trade in ivory

One thousand miles south of Socotra lay Saracen Madagascar, ruled by four sheiks. Marco reported that there were many elephants here and so there was a great trade in ivory. The country was covered by forests of sandal wood trees and amber was also plentiful here.

"I have been told gryphons come from this island. But they are not, as is commonly thought, half bird half lion, being rather like eagles, with a wing-span of thirty paces, strong enough to lift an elephant into the air," wrote Marco Polo, thus substituting a new myth for the legend of the fabulous gryphon.

Then he described Zanzibar and its people who were "tall and fat though they are not tall enough for their width. They are so large-limbed that they seem like giants and so strong that each one of them can carry a load big enough for four men. But this is nothing to marvel at for each of them eats as much as five people. They are all black-skinned with large mouths and flat noses, enormous eyes and curly hair . . .

"The women are more ugly than you can imagine. They have large mouths, short fat noses and enormous hands . . ."

But they were a very warlike people. Instead of horses, they rode to battle on camels and elephants, fighting with lances, swords and stones. Wooden turrets, holding twelve or more men, were set on the backs of elephants and the elephants were given wine to drink so that they would be more fierce. The wine was made out of rice, sugar and spices, and not grapes.

Apart from elephants there were many other animals to be found in this country. Marco Polo saw one kind he had never heard of before: "Their bodies are rather short and slope down towards the rear, because their hind-legs are somewhat shorter than the front legs which are very long, as are their necks. They do not harm anyone. Their skin is red and white in rings and they are a most attractive sight." He was describing the giraffe.

Another animal he described was the whale, which was hunted for the ambergris in its intestines. Ambergris is a blackish-gray fatty substance with a sweet earthy smell. It is used in Europe for making scent, but in the East it is also used as a medicine or flavoring agent in cooking.

"Middle India" consisted of a "large province" called Abyssinia which was ruled by a Christian king. Marco was told that six lesser kings ruled under him: three Christian and three Saracen.

The Christians were branded with three marks, one on the forehead and two on the cheeks, but the Saracens had only one mark which was on their foreheads. The Saracens lived near Aden where St. Thomas converted many people before he went to Coromandel.

There was obviously much friction between the Christian and the Saracen communities, as is shown in the following story.

The King of Abyssinia wanted to go on pilgrimage to the tomb of Christ, but because he would have had to pass through the hostile Saracen country round Aden, he sent a bishop in his place. The bishop made the journey safely but on his return was imprisoned by the Sultan of Aden, who tried to convert him to the Saracen faith. The bishop would not be converted, however, and so the Sultan had him branded as a Saracen and sent him back to Abyssinia.

When the King of Abyssinia found out what had been done to his bishop he "nearly died of grief," and declared that he would avenge the shame which had been put on him. At once he called together a vast army and moved against Aden. He laid waste the country and killed as many Saracens as he could. Then he returned home. This happened in 1288.

For the benefit of future merchants and seamen, Marco Polo mentioned that there was a good port in Aden from which small merchant vessels could travel down a large river for seven days. Then the merchants had to land and load their goods on camels. After traveling overland for thirty days they would reach the River Nile and, riding along the banks of this river, reach Alexandria itself.

At once the young man and the princess began to struggle with great vigor

Larger ships sailed from Aden to India, carrying horses which were greatly in demand there. The Sultan of Aden levied a tax on these ships and their merchandise, and this trade was so profitable that he became one of the richest rulers in the world.

In Shihr, four hundred miles from Aden, the camels, oxen, horses and rams of the people were fed on dried or fresh fish because there was no grass and the fishing was particularly good in these parts.

An incense made of resin was exported from a town called Dhofar, five hundred miles east of Shihr.

A fierce battle began, the cruelest that was ever seen

Marco Polo then went on to describe some of the other Mongol kingdoms he had heard of.

In Turkestan there lived a Khan called Kaidu. He was a very ambitious man and kept making war on the Great Khan, who was his uncle.

This Khan had a daughter called Ayaruk, which meant "Bright Moon." This princess was quite unlike other girls, for she was strongly built and loved fighting. She was so good at it, too, that no man had ever been able to triumph over her in a trial of strength.

It was very awkward for the Khan, her father. He wanted to marry her off and the princess refused to marry anyone who was weaker than herself. The princess was very stubborn about this and in the end her father had to give in and let her have her way.

A proclamation was sent out to the four corners of his kingdom asking any nobleman who wanted to try his strength against the princess to come to the court of the Khan. If he succeeded he should have the princess for his wife.

As soon as the news spread abroad noblemen came to the Khan's court from all parts of the world.

The contests took place in the great hall of the palace. The Khan, the queen and a great company of noblemen and women would come down to watch the

fight, and as soon as they were settled the princess would come in, dressed in a silk tunic, and the young challenger would stand up against her.

The agreement was that if he won the princess was to marry him, but if he lost the young man was to give her one hundred horses. Soon the princess had won a good ten thousand horses and this was hardly surprising, for she was so big and broadly built that she looked like a giantess.

One day, in 1280, a prince arrived at the court of Kaidu Khan. He was the son of the King of Pumar and had come to try his strength against the princess. He was a very handsome young man, who had never been defeated in any trial of strength. Frank of heart, and sure of victory, he came surrounded by a noble company, bringing a thousand horses with him as his stake in the trial of strength.

Everybody hoped that the princess had at last met her match, and when he saw him Kaidu Khan was delighted and longed for him to marry his daughter. He was so keen on the match that he even went to the princess and implored her to let herself be beaten. But the princess only said: "My father, I shall fight as always and let the stronger one win."

Then the princess came into the hall. At once the young man and the princess set to and began to struggle with great vigor. Alas, it was only a short time before the prince was forced to admit defeat, while all the bystanders mourned to see him vanquished. The thousand horses were given to the proud girl and the prince returned sadly to his own country.

Making the best of a bad job, Kaidu Khan often took his daughter into battle with him, and she would hurl herself so fiercely on the enemy that no knight, however strong he was, could resist her. She would simply pick him up and carry him off by force.

And so the beautiful princess Bright Moon never found a husband, but became famous as the most valiant soldier in the whole kingdom.

But in spite of his daughter, Kaidu Khan was one day cruelly defeated by Arghun Khan, the man to whom Niccolo, Maffeo and Marco Polo were supposed to be taking the Tartar princess. And this was how it came about.

The lands of Kaidu Khan bordered those of Abagha Khan, the father of Arghun, near a region called "the Solitary Tree." Fearing that Kaidu Khan might raid his lands, Abagha Khan sent Prince Arghun with a large army of horsemen and infantry to guard the borders of his kingdom.

When Kaidu Khan heard of this he at once sent his brother, a brave nobleman called Barak, to fight Prince Arghun, and soon the two armies were face to face. The trumpets rang out and a fierce battle began, the cruelest that was ever seen. Both sides fought hard, but in the end Barak and his army began to retreat and at last they fled in disorder, leaving Arghun victorious.

But he was not able to enjoy his victory for long. Shortly after the battle, Arghun received news that his father was dead and, full of sorrow, he returned to take over the lordship of Persia, which was a good forty days' journey away.

Now it so happened that the brother of the dead Abagha Khan reached the kingdom before Arghun could take possession of it. Seizing the treasure in the state coffers, he bribed all the chief nobles of the kingdom to support him in claiming the crown. Then, when he heard that Arghun was approaching with a large army to win back his father's throne, he called together a vast host and marched against Arghun.

The two armies camped facing each other on a good plain, and before the battle began the two leaders addressed their troops.

The uncle, who was a sultan and had been converted to the Saracen religion, promised that he would give his soldiers all the spoils which they might win in the fight against Arghun.

Arghun, on the other hand, heartened his troops to fight against the sultan who had taken the kingdom from its rightful successor, and reminded them that the sultan was a Muslim and therefore not fit to rule over a Christian people.

Then one of Arghun's supporters suggested that, before coming to grips with so strong an enemy, ambassadors should be sent to the sultan to try for a peaceful agreement. This was done. But the sultan replied:

"Go back to Arghun and report to him that I will accept him as my nephew and son, in accordance with my duty, and that I will further grant him one part of the state. But I shall not let him have the crown. If he does not accept these terms, tell him to prepare for battle."

When Arghun heard this reply, he realized that nothing further could be done and at once he gave the signal to attack.

The battle was fought with great bravery on both sides. Arghun and his soldiers fought valiantly but they had little chance against such odds. They were defeated and the prince was taken prisoner. Immediately after the battle, the sultan put his captive nephew in charge of a general called Melik and left the battlefield.

Now it happened that a Tartar prince, who was in the sultan's army, began to grow angry that the rightful king should be a helpless prisoner, and the more he thought

Arghun Khan was taken prisoner

about it the angrier he became. So he set about talking to the other princes and little by little he gradually persuaded them to return to Arghun's side. When this had been accomplished they went to Arghun's prison and set him free. They told him that they were sorry they had been disloyal to him and begged him to forgive them. Arghun was only too happy to become reconciled to them. Then they went to Melik's pavilion, killed the general who was in charge and proclaimed Arghun the lord of the Tartars.

When the sultan learned that his general was dead and that the Tartar princes had recognized Arghun as their lord, he tried to flee with the few supporters who remained faithful to him. But a prince, who was a friend of Arghun and had been ordered to guard one of the mountain passes, recognized the sultan as he rode up. He came to meet him, took him prisoner after a short struggle and brought him before Arghun.

Arghun at once ordered him to be put to death as a traitor. Then he sent his own son with thirty thousand horsemen to guard the borders of his kingdom.

This was how Arghun Khan became ruler of the Persian Tartars. All this took place in 1285. Arghun reigned for six years before he was poisoned, and died just before Niccolo, Maffeo and Marco Polo arrived, bringing the Mongol princess to his court.

After his death one of his uncles succeeded to the throne, for his son was far away on the borders of the kingdom. The uncle reigned for two years, then he, too, died of poison.

The northern lands

When he had written this account of Persia, Marco turned to the lands of the far north and wrote down what he had heard about them.

North of the Caspian Sea lay the kingdom of the White Horde, whose king, Konchi, was descended from Genghis Khan. He ruled over a primitive Mongol population who lived a nomadic life on the plains and in the mountains as their ancestors had done.

They worshiped Natigai, making felt images of him and offering food to him so that he would protect their lands and goods. But unlike the Mongol tribes of Genghis Khan they were a peace-loving people.

In this land of lakes and swamps and vast expanses of ice there were many large white bears, black foxes, wild asses and sables: "those animals," said Marco, "whose skins are so valuable that one man's fur coat costs a thousand besants."

Further north lay a country called the "Dark Valley"

(One gold besant was then worth about one dollar and seventy-five cents.)

It was hard to travel through this wild country and Marco Polo explained that dogs were used to draw heavy "sledges without wheels for wheels would sink to the bottom of the mud or slide about on the ice." The traveler sat on a bearskin which was laid on the sleigh and each sledge was drawn by six dogs "who know the road so well that they can go from one posting station to the next without being directed." There was a posting station at the end of each day's journey.

The people who lived in this country were good huntsmen and trappers.

Still further north lay a country which Marco Polo called the "Dark Valley." "Here the sun never shines and the moon and stars are never seen, for a perpetual darkness lies over the land."

The inhabitants of this region were pale-skinned and led very primitive lives. When the Mongols went on hunting expeditions there they took some mares and their foals with them. They would cave the foals on the borders of the Dark Valley, moving into the country with the mares. When they had finished hunting and

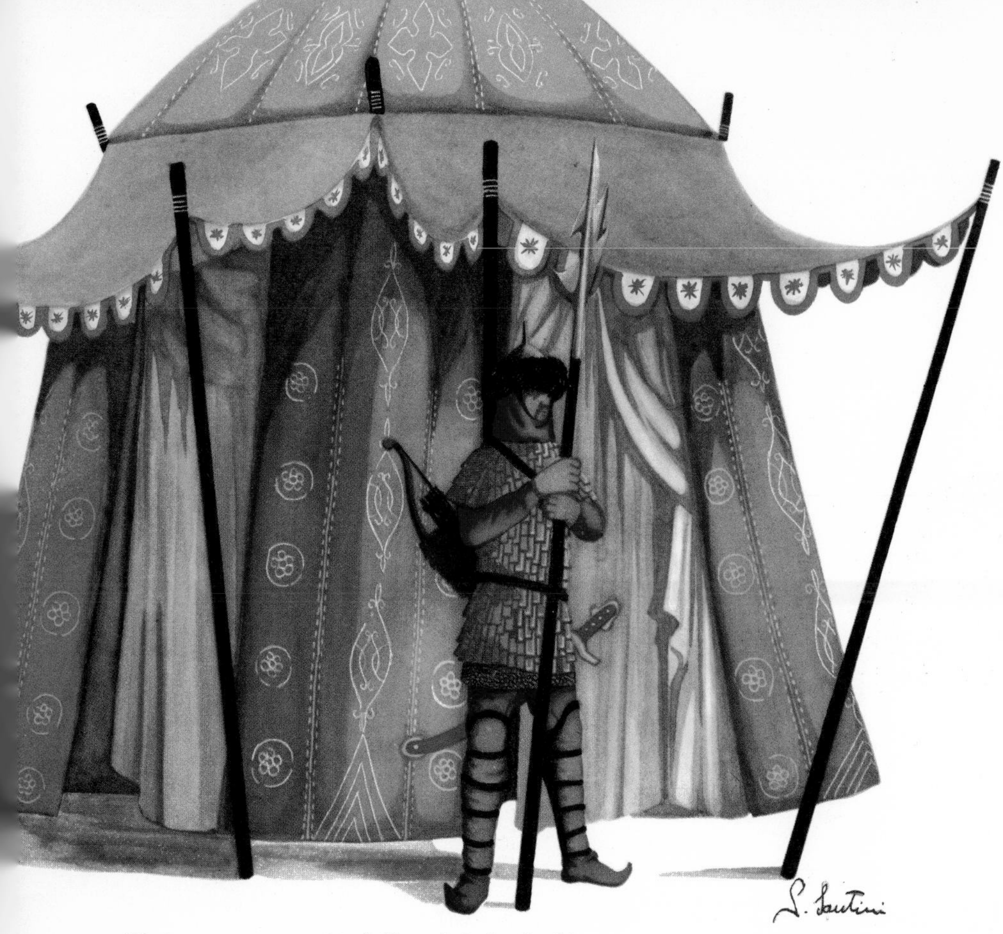
Their tents were made of silk and cloth of gold

wanted to find their way back, they would give the horses their heads and they would instinctively run towards their foals, thus guiding the huntsmen back to their starting point.

Marco Polo also gave a brief description of Russia. "The climate here is also very cold. The inhabitants are Christians of the Greek Church and pay tribute to the Tartar Khan of the Golden Horde. They are a tall, fair-haired people, very handsome in appearance and wear simple clothes. They trap animals for fur and extract silver from the many mines. It is not far from Russia to Norway but because of the extremely cold climate it is impossible to travel there . . ."

Between the River Oxus and the Black Sea lay the kingdom of the northern Mongols called the Golden Horde, whose first Khan, Batu Sain, overran most of Russia, Lac, Hungary, Circassia and the Crimea. A descendant of this Khan ruled over them in Marco's day. His name was Toktai.

Towards the end of his account of Khubilai Khan and his Mongol empire, Marco Polo described the battle which had taken place in 1261 between Barka, Lord of the Western Mongols, and Hulagu, Khan of the Mongols of Persia. This arose over a dispute, each party claiming possession of the same province. After preparing for six months, they rode against each other. Each had an army of more than three hundred thousand horsemen. When they pitched camp, on the night before the battle, their tents, made of silk and cloth of gold, were a most splendid sight to behold.

On the morning of the battle, Barka led thirty-five battalions of ten thousand men into the field. Hulagu had only three hundred thousand men. They chose a vast plain on which to fight because their armies were so great. All the soldiers were brave and eager, and both the leaders were descended from Genghis Khan.

When both sides were ready the drums began to sound, and soon the air was thick with arrows. When the archers had used all their arrows the battlefield was covered with dead and wounded. Then the horsemen swept down over the field with swords in their hands slashing at each other until "so many heads, arms and hands flew up into the air that it was a wonder to behold. I am sure that never before have so many people been killed on a battlefield. Blood flowed everywhere; the horses pawed the ground, up to their hocks in blood and the cries of the wounded were enough to pierce every heart."

Hulagu Khan fought like a storm-wind. Nobody could stand against the ferocity of his charge for long, and at last, Barka Khan, in spite of his larger army, was forced to flee. For a time Hulagu Khan and his men pursued the enemy, killing as many of the retreating soldiers as they could. Then he returned to camp and ordered that the bodies of friend and foe alike should be burned in accordance with custom.

Marco Polo had now almost finished writing his famous book. In the prison in Genoa, where he spent the three years from 1296 to 1299, he wrote the final words:

"I have now told you about the Mongols and their customs, and about all the countries in Asia except for those around the Black Sea, for those are already well-known to the merchants of Venice, Pisa, Genoa and other places.

"I have told you how we took our leave of the Great Khan, a thing that was by no means easy; and if the chance to accompany King Arghun's bride had not come our way, we would probably never have returned to our own country.

"But it was God's will that we should return, so that we could describe the marvelous things which there are in the world. For there has certainly never been a Christian, Saracen or Mongol who has explored so much of the world as Messer Marco Polo, son of Messer Niccolo Polo, noble citizen of Venice. Thanks be to God.

Amen."